WOMEN
AND
WAR

"At first glance, Russia's war in Ukraine could be seen as yet another territorial invasion. For millennia, man has always wanted more. More land, more power. However, what is currently being played out in this country has much more the hallmarks of an ideological struggle, at the heart of which lies the fateful question: 'Do we have the right to choose what we want to be?' It's all about free will—be it political (joining the EU), cultural (speaking Ukrainian) or sexual (not being heterosexual). This book is the story of thirty Ukrainian women who have decided to choose what they want to become, and it will grip and inspire you from first page to last."

—*Stephen Fry*

"I read this collection of powerful and intimate letters from Ukrainian women as an antidote to the news and polemics that reduce lives to politics and statistics. These stories will move you and haunt you; they will uplift and inspire you; they will break your heart and then put it back together again as you listen to women struggling to survive yet another terrible man-made catastrophe."

—*Lana Wachowski,*
American director and screenwriter (*The Matrix*)

"*Women and War* shatters the traditional image of war. Since the Russian invasion of 2022, Ukrainian women have been more than witnesses - they are fighters, caretakers, fundraisers and fierce pillars of resistance. This moving collection tells their stories and shows that true strength and courage know no gender."

—*Mstyslav Chernov,*
Ukrainian journalist, filmmaker, war correspondent, and Oscar winner
(*20 Days in Mariupol*)

"This is an extraordinary and essential book. The origins and consequences of the war in Ukraine have been analyzed in many ways: geopolitics, histories, cultures, identities. The war is also, as all wars are, deeply personal. To make sense of the war is not just to explain it, but to try to feel it through an act of empathy. In this book are personal stories of fear, hatred, and love in the face of injustice, cruelty, and violence. This book helps us to understand the range of emotions that underpin the will of the Ukrainian people to fight, resist, and overcome. Only through the first-person narration of these Ukrainian women can we truly understand what this war means to the individuals who are living it."

—*Professor Rawi Abdelal,*
Herbert F. Johnson Professor of International Management,
Harvard Business School

WOMEN AND WAR

Letters from Ukraine to the Free World

Aurélie Bros

BOSTON
2025

Library of Congress Cataloging-in-Publication Data

Names: Bros, Aurélie compiler
Title: Women and war : letters from Ukraine to the free world / Aurélie Bros.
Other titles: Wie ein Lichtstrahl in der Finsternis. English | Letters from Ukraine to the free world
Description: Boston : Cherry Orchard Books, 2025. | Originally published in German as "Wie ein Lichtstrahl in der Finsternis: Briefe von Frauen aus der Ukraine an die freie Welt."
Identifiers: LCCN 2025010200 (print) | LCCN 2025010201 (ebook) | ISBN 9798887198224 hardback | ISBN 9798887198194 paperback | ISBN 9798887198200 adobe pdf | ISBN 9798887198217 epub
Subjects: LCSH: Russo-Ukrainian War, 2014---Women--Ukraine | Women and war--Ukraine | Women--Ukraine--Correspondence
Classification: LCC DK5529.W66 W5413 2025 (print) | LCC DK5529.W66 (ebook) | DDC 947.706/21082--dc23/eng/20250404
LC record available at https://lccn.loc.gov/2025010200
LC ebook record available at https://lccn.loc.gov/2025010201

Copyright © Academic Studies Press, 2025, English translation
First published in German as *"Wie ein Lichtstrahl in der Finsternis": Briefe von Frauen aus der Ukraine an die freie Welt* by Elisabeth Sandmann Verlag GmbH, Munich 2023;
ISBN 978 394 958 223.
Copyright © 2023 Elisabeth Sandmann Verlag GmbH

Book design by Lapiz Business Solutions
On the cover: photograph of Dina Yong by Anastasia Potapova

Published by Cherry Orchard Books, an imprint of Academic Studies Press
1007 Chestnut Street
Newton, MA 02464, USA
www.academicstudiespress.com

To the Ukrainian people.

To all those who are committed to defending freedom.

To Éden and Elizabeth.

Contents

Introduction	xi
Olga Stefanyshyna	1
Sofiia O.	5
Olena Bilozerska	10
Mariana Motrunych	14
Iryna Novokreshchenova	25
Mariia Lepokhina, aka Masha Syta	30
Olha Boravlova	35
Jerry Heil	45
Ira Solomatina	51
Mariia Cherpak	54
Sofiia Kropyvnytska	59
Yana Nakonechna	63
Adelina Mokliak	70
Olga Afanasyeva	77
Anastasiya Gruba	84
Iryna Chernychenko	89
Kristina Parioti	95
Anastasia Selevanova	102
Oksana L.	106
Olha Olshanska	110
Maryna Kamenskaya	118
Kateryna Vozianova	126
Taïsia Klochko	136

Oksana Korchynska	141
Yuliia Paievska, aka Tayra	147
Sophia Podkolsina	150
Meriam Yol	163
Dina Vong	169
Hannah Marholina	184
Kateryna Iakovlenko	191
Emily Channell-Justice	195
Oleksandra Matviichuk	206
Acknowledgements	210

Introduction

March 3, 2025

If a war were to break out in your home country tomorrow, what would you do about it? Would you leave your grandparents and parents to face an uncertain future to take your children to safety abroad? Would you donate part of your salary to support your army? Or would you join up straight away, go to the front line and risk your life? Would you stay in your beloved home when your city is occupied, knowing that the enemy could rape or execute you for no reason? On the contrary, would you leave everything you own to start a new life as a refugee somewhere else, in a place you don't know, a language you don't speak and where you have no friends? If your husband was killed by the invader while trying to protect your country, would you have the strength to continue raising your children?

There is no immediate answer. However, on February 24, 2022, the Ukrainian women were backed into a corner. With limited time to carefully consider all the aspects of each question, they were required to decide immediately.

For those of you who were fortunate enough to grow up in a peaceful country, the concepts of invasion and war may be difficult to fathom. You may think of the history books and novels that you have read, or the movies and pictures that you have seen, but there is still something abstract about it. After all, it is difficult to understand what we have not personally experienced.

As the full invasion began, Ukraine began to make headlines. The problem is that people can get used to even the most horrific crimes, such as attacks on civilians, hitting homes, hospitals, kindergartens and schools; the use of cluster munitions, which are banned by many international conventions; the targeting of humanitarian corridors; or even the execution of prisoners of war. The drama is slowly fading. We risk forgetting that Russia is behind it all, will not stop, and that Moscow's thirst for land and power could make you its next victim, having decided to attack Ukraine to challenge the world order and regain the power of a bygone era.

If I were, however, to tell you the story of little Nastia, a ten-year-old orphan from Mariupol who lived in a basement for a month, ate soup made from water drawn from radiators, and had to evacuate the city after her cat was burnt alive in the bombing of her apartment by Russian forces, you would have a different reaction. You would think of Nastia in the evening as you hugged your children after work. You might even think of her when you see a Ukrainian flag on the street and ask yourself: 'Where is she right now? Is she okay?' You may even wonder what you can do to help put an end to this horror.

Behind figures are the faces and stories of ordinary people like you and me, torn from their peaceful daily lives. It is these stories that I wanted to publish, not to stop the conflict (that would be very naive), but to help us to feel a real empathy with the Ukrainian people who have lived through eleven years of war, including three years of full-scale invasion. As I write these words, the fourth year of invasion and the twelfth year of war have just begun.

As Oleksandra Matviichuk, the 2022 Peace Nobel Laureate, has expressed on numerous occasions, it is of paramount importance to prioritize the human dimension in any discourse. I would add that it is necessary to restore humanity and courage to our hearts—we citizens of the free world who have forgotten that freedom requires critical thinking, while it is based on individual responsibility, political engagement, and the defense of truth and resistance to authoritarian tendencies.

This book portrays a people fighting for their freedom. Thirty women (ranging in age from 10 to 72) took up the offer to share their inner thoughts and feelings with us. Despite a significant loss of territory, a life in constant fear of catastrophe as Russia even targets nuclear power stations or drones attack cities every night, and a cruel daily routine as even schools and hospitals are bombed, they will not give up. These women believe in democracy, human rights, religious freedom, the rule of law, social justice, cultural pluralism, environmental awareness and self-expression.

I hope that reading these life stories will help you understand Ukrainians who need our help more than ever—and also inspire us. If we, the West, do not take action, the consequences will be felt for a long time. The fall of Ukraine will not just be theirs; it will be a huge crack in our shared world, allowing authoritarian darkness to spread. None of us will be safe. It will be a world where the stories of the protagonists in this book could become the story of every woman in the free world. It could be the future of your colleague, neighbor, friend, mother, sister, or daughter. Just think for a moment of your beloved daughter or niece going through the kind of hell that little Nastia went through.

Like all books, this one has an origin story. In early March 2022, Germany's leading financial newspaper, *Handelsblatt*, offered me the opportunity to run a program to help Ukrainian journalists in need. I soon met extraordinary people whose lives had been turned upside down when the first bombing raids ended their normal pre-war lives. The stories I heard were not only heartbreaking, but also powerful. Parents driving desperately for days to get children—their own and others—to safety. Couples separated by war embracing at the border, wondering if this is the last time they will ever have the chance to do so.

Not surprisingly, the burden of mortality fell mainly on the men who went off to fight. Women, on the other hand, returned—whether they wanted to or not—to their traditional role as the guardians of the family, with all the workload that entailed. It was the women who fascinated me most, because they became more emancipated and began to challenge the conventional discourse on gender and were ready to participate wholeheartedly in the war effort.

In June 2022, I decided to collect these stories to highlight the paradox of war. Courage is born in the worst of times. Love grows stronger in lands ravaged by death. Humanity always shines through the darkness of horror. That is why I decided to ask these women to write letters.

Facing a blank page is a bit like having a heart-to-heart conversation with yourself. Alone with your conscience, you can say what is not easily verbalized. It is a cleansing that brings spiritual renewal and release from pain. It is also an opportunity to look forward to the future.

As word spread, more and more women were willing to share their experiences and talk about how they longed for freedom. Artists, businesswomen, politicians, teachers, and soldiers contacted me. When I least expected it, children wrote to me. They too wanted to talk about the disaster that had robbed them of their innocence.

Some older women, all in their 80s, refused to participate in the book. Let me give you some details of their stories, because silence sometimes speaks volumes. There was an old grandmother; let's call her Ludmila. At first, she was tempted to tell her poignant story, but in the end, she decided to remain silent. She was afraid of endangering her family. She had been brought up in the Soviet Union, a time when the expression of feelings in public was dangerous.

I experienced the same reaction from Clara, an elderly Jewish woman from Mariupol who sent me a heartbreaking letter about the daily life of a grandmother with diabetes. It was a description of how Russian soldiers were cold-bloodedly killing civilians in the streets for no reason. She explained the difficulty of climbing the five floors of her flat without a lift and confessed that she had stopped eating for several days so that her sick husband could survive. Just before this book was published, she begged me to take the letter out. Her husband thought she had made a terrible mistake and that family members could be executed by the Russians as punishment. It was then that I understood the extent to which the generation that had grown up under Stalin was still traumatized by the repression of a totalitarian regime. These women thought the project was dangerous and preferred to remain silent. Given the cruelty of the Russian army, these fears are all too justified.

Yelena, a lady in her late 90s, loved the idea of the book, but in the end she decided not to take part. She said that writing would have forced her to remember the horrors of the twentieth century: the Stalinist purges; the Second World War; a husband who works in the mines of the Donbas; and the 1990s with its financial turmoil and endemic corruption. She was not ready to look back. She told me that she would so much like to leave this planet in peace, surrounded by her loved ones, but she did not want to leave knowing what Russia would do to her grandchildren and great-grandchildren.

Looking at the list of women who share their letters in this book, it is clear that most of them are young, white, educated, and often from privileged backgrounds. You would rightly point out that my choice of protagonists does not represent the diversity of Ukraine's ethnicities, religions, and cultures. Try as I might, I could not really change that. How do you convince these traumatized old ladies to write about their experiences? If you come from an underrepresented background, how can you trust an unknown woman when your life has taught you that survival depends on privacy? In the end, I gave up. I would have liked to have had a more in-depth look at the diversity of Ukrainian society, but the format of these letters was not the right one for that project, which is important in its own right.

One morning I received a letter, then two, then three, and so on. Reading about these horrors in the calm of a safe city was a disturbing experience. I often interrupted my lecture to watch my daughter play, aware of the fragility of the peace we enjoyed. My thoughts were with the Ukrainian soldiers fighting for them, their country and, in a way, all of us.

My partner, my daughter, and I were here in Berlin, far from the explosions, by a twist of fate. I was not forced to leave my loved one at the border to protect my child in a country whose language I did not speak. I did not have to leave my parents in the hope that some volunteer would bring them food. I have never been forced to stand in line with my fellow countrymen and women for nappies and clean clothes. I had none of that because I was the winner of the birth lottery.

So please read the letters with an open heart. Through their vulnerability and trust in love, these women embody their country with absolute authenticity. Their stories are a record of life during a war, and in the pages that follow you will discover kisses that taste of tears, songs of hope that are punctuated by sobs, and loves that do not know if they will have a future. Listen to their voices, voices that come together to express the will of a people to win, to heal their wounds, and to mourn their dead. As the Ukrainian folk song "Oy u vyshnevomu sadochku" says so well, let them build a future when . . .

>In the orchards of cherry trees,
>We will hear the nightingales sing.

Note on the text

Most of the letters below were written in Ukrainian, while some were written in Russian and English. The translation into English was done by Aurélie Bros. Ellipses in the letters are original; the letters have not been edited in any way.

This collection was first published as: *"Wie ein Lichtstrahl in der Finsternis"*: *Briefe von Frauen aus der Ukraine an die freie Welt* by Elisabeth Sandmann Verlag GmbH, Munich/Germany 2023; ISBN 978 394 958 223. Copyright © 2023 Elisabeth Sandmann Verlag GmbH

By Olga Stefanyshyna

Date of birth: May 14, 1983
From: Kyiv
Profession: Member of the Verkhovna Rada, Ukrainian Parliament (Deputy Minister of Health from 2018 to 2019)
In Kyiv at the start of the invasion

August 01, 2022

My life ended on February 24.

Since that day, I've never slept in my own bed—the one my husband Bohdan and I had chosen to live happily together. He was killed on March 30 by a Russian shell during a humanitarian mission near the Ukrainian town of Chernihiv. At the time, all hell was breaking loose there, and he and his comrades were rescuing people from the Russian occupiers. Previously, they had brought over 150 people to safety in Butcha and Irpin. But that day, their convoy was spotted by an enemy drone and a mortar hit them. Bohdan was killed in a split second: the damned shell hit him head-on. All our guys wanted to do was distribute food and water to the inhabitants of the occupied territories and evacuate those who wanted to escape the misery...

Imagine that one day you no longer live in your apartment, where you've spent tens of thousands of happy hours with your family. August has already arrived, but there's still a dusty Christmas tree under which real miracles happened on Christmas Eve: parents and children and all your friends unwrapped their presents. Everyone got their wish. The adults drank champagne, the children threw confetti. You allowed them to do this in the apartment because, after all, it's a symbol of New Year's joy. At the time, you thought the happiness was so dense, that you could have eaten it with a spoon, so saturated was the air in the apartment with it. You loved it so much. And today, you're not sure you'll ever be able to experience it again. Just imagine. As history has shown, no one in the world is immune to suffering like war, which takes away everything you love in a second. Forever.

Today, Russia is not at war with Ukraine. It is at war with the entire civilized world. It has been for many years, and this war has now reached its climax. I am personally grateful to all those who have helped Ukraine during these bloody months. But I have one big request: we need more powerful weapons, and we need them as soon as possible. Because every day that passes costs the lives of our best people and the lost dreams of our young children.

We were a very happy family. Thirteen years of marriage and two wonderful daughters, Vlada and Valeria, aged thirteen and ten. Our home was full of harmony, we loved cooking delicious meals and inviting friends over. We were cheerful and enjoyed simple things.

Bohdan has always been my support. I'm a workaholic by nature and have worked for over fifteen years in various projects and social organizations. I defended the rights of seriously ill people in need of treatment and fought against corruption. At one time, I founded a powerful advocacy organization called "Patients of Ukraine" whose aim is to help the sick and now wounded of the Russian-Ukrainian war. After the Revolution of Dignity in 2014, my colleagues and I launched a reform of Ukraine's healthcare sector and, in 2018, I was lucky enough to become deputy to the best minister of health, Ulana Suprun, and implement this reform

alongside her. Three years ago, I was elected to the Verkhovna Rada of Ukraine, the Ukrainian parliament, where I successfully defended health-related issues. I know that thanks to my work and leadership, tens of thousands of people have received essential medicines and medical care. One of the reasons for my success is the support of my husband Bohdan. He always encouraged me to achieve new things, was my compass, and was proud of what I was doing for the country.

Today, I'm proud of him. Because he died for this country. He died a true hero, saving people from the misery caused by the Russians. Unfortunately, I'm proud of him with tears of sorrow in my eyes and a huge wound in my heart.

He loved me and the girls very much, but he always said that Ukraine came first.

This was no idle talk. He'd learned that from his father from an early age. They were his words. All his life, Yevhen, Bohdan's father, spoke of the terrible danger posed by Russia and was a fervent patriot. Bohdan's grandparents were members of the UPA (Ukrainian Insurgent Army). For this reason, Yevhen's father (Bohdan's grandfather) was killed by Chekists, and his wife Stefa was sent to a concentration camp in Solovki. Their young son Yevhen was exiled to Siberia with his grandparents. The trauma of the Soviet regime remained engraved in Yevhen's memory for the rest of his life. Bohdan's father burned all documents attesting to their family's stay in the Soviet camps. He wanted to save his children from the genocide perpetrated by the Russian authorities. But the love of Ukraine was firmly rooted in his son's heart: he was ready to die for his homeland. After all, Yevhen often said: "The time will come when Russia will wage a great bloody war against Ukraine. But we will survive and we will win, and the whole world will know and be proud of Ukraine, and our flags will fly in every corner of the world.

If we trace a family history, we see that history repeats itself. Bloody massacres, murder, and torture of the innocent—this is what Russia has been doing to Ukraine (and not only Ukraine) for centuries. Less than a hundred years ago, Bohdan's grandfather gave his life for Ukraine, and today, his grandson has been killed by Rashists.

The last time I saw Bohdan was on March 24. I knew he was going to a dangerous place near Chernihiv to save people because, at the time, horror reigned there. Friends told me it was very risky and that maybe I shouldn't let him do it. "Are you sure you should do it now?" I asked him. "I can't not do it," he replied. I still remember his blue eyes and his firm assurance. That's heroism—his personal heroism and that of our nation. We protect our people, our land, and, above all, our identity, because we have to. Please help us to ensure that no other nation in the civilized world has to feel what I and millions of Ukrainians are feeling right now. We must defeat Russia. All together.

[Author's note: Olga still sits in parliament. One of her daughters went to study in the United Kingdom and the other stayed in Kyiv with Rocky, the dog they adopted.]

By Sofiia O.

Date of birth: September 18, 1997
From: the Luhans'k region
Profession: Community manager
(former history student)
First exposure to war: 2014
In Kyiv at the start of the invasion

July 24, 2022

To date, Russia's war against Ukraine has lasted five months. For five months, eight years, and a few centuries, Ukrainians have been fighting for their freedom, their independence, their history and culture, for their own path to development. Russia, for its part, is drowning in its own stubbornness, repeating: you are Mazepians, Petliurians, Banderists, nationalists and fascists, collective farmers, Lenin invented you, you simply don't exist. Russia is interfering in the internal affairs of a neighboring country, trying not only to impose its policies but also to seize, conquer, and destroy certain regions. It talks of independence, but never forgets its imperial ambitions.

Today, many people are mistaken about the start date of Russia's war against Ukraine. It's not February 24, 2022. This war began with Crimea and Donbas. This war began when I was sixteen and a foreign army suddenly appeared on the streets of my hometown.

In 2014, I was finishing my tenth year in a small town in the far east of Ukraine. It was twenty-three kilometers from the Russian border and forty kilometers from Luhans'k. My family always spoke Russian, my parents' parents lived in Russia, but I went to Ukrainian school, we read texts by Taras Shevchenko, Vassyl Simonenko, and Mykola Khvyliovy in class and we always supported the Ukrainian national football team. In sixteen years, I've never heard anyone say that we should belong to Russia or that Donbas wasn't part of Ukraine.

I don't remember my reaction to the annexation of Crimea, the start of the Anti-Terrorist Operation Zone, the pseudo-referendum, and the proclamation of any republics. My ordinary life as a teenager hasn't changed at all. The school curriculum, the eight hours of Ukrainian language lessons, and the blue and yellow flag above the school remained the same. Everything was business as usual. I'm ashamed of it, but at the time, I only perceived my country's tragedy as a subject for discussion with adults (which makes you grow old), as another game of "politics" where, in the end, everyone gets away with it and nothing terrible happens. I followed the events in Sloviansk as if they didn't concern me, as if they were happening on the other side of the world. While I was volunteering at a preschool camp, my mother came to see me at my school for the first time in years, in the middle of a working day and told me I had to go and get my things, which was an absolute shock to me. The fighting was coming.

Over the summer of 2014, I came to three important conclusions through sheer force of circumstance:

1) Knowledge is power. It can prepare you for the worst scenarios, it prevents you from being deceived, and it doesn't leave you confused. From this point of view, choosing to study history was a very good choice, this aspect was one of the reasons why I enrolled.
2) There's no point in judging people who have never heard the sound of a grenade exploding and who don't demonstrate "correct understanding." This was the main lesson I took with me to Kyiv when I started studying there in 2015. I now remember this lesson when I talk to Europeans who sometimes find it hard to understand how Ukrainians feel.
3) The combination of naivety and hope can cause great pain. I remember waking up in August 2014 and my first thought was, "Not much longer, and Ukrainian forces will take back these territories." Every morning, hope is reborn, but in the evening it turns into a nightmare with no end in sight.

For the next year, until August 2015, I lived under occupation. I have to say that my city was still intact, my loved ones were alive and well, and it was a very different kind of occupation from 2022—with no reprisals or filtration camps. But I was seventeen and, of course, my worries seemed the height of tragedy. Why had we been abandoned and why weren't they continuing to fight for us? How could I graduate from high school and start college under occupation? Why did this happen to me?

I'm very grateful to my parents and teachers who did everything they could so that my classmates and I could obtain Ukrainian papers, pass the necessary exams, and start studying. My mother and my history teacher, who became a real mentor to me, had come out of the occupied territory under the bombardments into Ukrainian territory, negotiated with the military, and made it possible for me and the others to get out and study.

In 2015, I went to Kyiv, made friends, and saw my parents every six months. And I started writing a research paper on the history of the Chechen war. I tried to understand, to intellectualize my own experiences, and to find an answer to the question of why things are the way they are, and why Russia keeps trying to kill all life around it. I've studied Russian history and answered the question of why I'm doing this a hundred times: because it's at war with my country. Even though millions of my compatriots didn't want Russia to be wiped off the map either. I remembered that knowledge is power. I know what Russian soldiers are capable of, I know what filtration camps are and what clean-up operations in cities look like, what it means when the Russian army "liberates" a city by first razing it to the ground. The whole world has seen what Russia has done time and time again but has refused to say so openly.

February 24, 2022, was not for me a shock like June 2014. Despite all the declarations from the international community, it was clear from the general tensions since the spring of 2021 that the use of chemical weapons, the closure of all independent media, and the bloodthirsty rhetoric were signs of preparation for something even more monstrous. Russia was preparing for a great war.

During my seven years in Kyiv, I often told my friends about the emergency kit, how the bathroom and the hallway were the safest rooms, how the grenade launchers fired, and how terrible it was to be shot at. I always told it in a happy tone, with a *happy ending* in sight: "Here I am, I'm alive, my parents are alive, I'm here and I'm laughing with you guys. Everything's going to be fine. I thought my friends would never see all this with their own eyes. In this case, even knowing didn't stop me from being naive and hopeful.

My parents stayed in my hometown. They never supported Russia's crimes and never believed in the "Russian world." I know that in Donbas, as in Crimea, there are still many people just waiting to go home. They are waiting for this land to be returned to Ukraine. Unfortunately, some of them won't see it, because Russia has killed them with its missiles or forced them into the army, where they have been used as cannon fodder.

I'm writing this from Kyiv, and I want to keep hoping. I want to see the blue and yellow flag in my school, where there are still so many good teachers who have nothing to do with the criminal regime. I want to see my parents more than once a year. I want Ukraine to win, I want us not to build our future under the sound of air raid sirens. I believe that knowledge will overcome naivety and that people will stop justifying evil simply because they don't know any better.

By Olena Bilozerska

Date of birth: August 5, 1979
Place of residence: Kyiv
Profession: Military officer in the Ukrainian armed forces. Journalist before the start of the war (2004-2014)
First encounter with war: 2014
In Kyiv at the start of the invasion

July 1, 2022

My name is Olena Bilozerska, and I was born in Kyiv into a family of engineers. I'm my parents' only child.

I've been interested in literature and poetry ever since I was a child. I've often been ill, so I've missed a lot of school, but I've always been an excellent student.

My mother tongue was Russian from a very early age, like all those of my generation who grew up in the big cities (except for western Ukraine, where Ukrainian has always been spoken). Indeed, during the one hundred years of Russian occupation, Ukraine became very Russified. When the Soviet Union collapsed and Ukraine became independent, I was twelve years old. In my childhood, Ukraine and Ukrainians were never spoken of in public as something separate from Russia, and most Ukrainians couldn't imagine that we'd get our own state so quickly and easily, without bloodshed. As it turned out, this was not the case. State independence is paid for in blood—if not now, then in the next generation, as happened to us.

I consciously switched to Ukrainian as an adult for patriotic reasons. In public, I write and speak only Ukrainian. But in everyday life, I still often speak Russian and listen to Russian songs. Russian rock and singer-songwriters—the music I've loved since I was young. I know and appreciate Russian poetry. This is the fate of the intellectuals of my generation. The next generation won't know all that and will speak Russian as a foreign language at best.

After completing my studies in literature, I tried my hand at journalism for a few years and was very successful. For ten years, I was a relatively well-known reporter and publicist, covering patriotic actions and protests in Kyiv with texts, photos, and videos. Under Yanukovych's pro-Russian regime, I was persecuted as an opposition journalist, and criminal cases were fabricated against me. But public opinion—both Ukrainian and foreign—came to my defense, and I saw for myself how effective public solidarity can be. Alongside my work as a journalist, I was also a human rights activist.

During those ten years, from 2004 to 2014, I was a member of a Ukrainian patriotic military sports organization, in which we were trained in the event of a Russian invasion. We familiarized ourselves with the basics of the army, learned tactics for moving in small groups, organizing ambushes, and so on. Our trainers were veterans of various local wars that had taken place on the territory of the former USSR in the 1990s. At the time, I had no idea that Russia would actually attack, that war would become a reality for all of us, let alone that it would be me, a woman with obviously inadequate training, who would have to fight. I saw our training as a hobby, an interesting pastime in the open air. At the same time, all those who took part in the training were ready to go to the front immediately if Russia really attacked. And that's what happened.

In the spring of 2014, when the war began (and not on February 24, 2022, eight years later), Russia only stopped spreading the lie that the people of Donbas, supposedly unhappy with Kyiv's policies, would fight us. It openly attacked us. In the spring of 2014, I was already in eastern Ukraine. For the first three and a half years, I fought as a sniper in the Ukrainian Volunteer Corps and the Ukrainian Volunteer Army. At the time, these informal units were not part of the official Ukrainian armed forces. We received no pay or compensation in the event of injury or death. Food, clothing, and equipment were provided by civilians who wanted to help at the front. In Ukraine, we call these people volunteers. In Western European languages, volunteers are people who do something of their own free will, helping others, whether civilians or soldiers. In Ukrainian, another usage developed during the war, where there are two different terms for "volunteers." A "volunteer" is not only a civilian who helps those on the front line but also someone who fights voluntarily. In Ukrainian, these two concepts are quite distinct. So we were voluntary fighters. And even though we received orders and ammunition from army commanders, we were still "illegally" on the front line, and often had to conceal our presence on the enemy's line of contact. That's why the documentary book I wrote and published about this period is called *Diary of an Underground Soldier*. It was published in two editions, nominated for the Shevchenko Prize, Ukraine's highest literary distinction, and even made the shortlist. By the way, Russians hate and fear all Ukrainian volunteer fighters and call them "Nazis." They also know me well from before the war and "love" me, often presenting me on TV as the greatest of all Ukrainian "Nazis."

So for three and a half years, from 2014 to 2017, I fought as an unregistered volunteer. As a sniper, I have more than ten confirmed successes. I always knew, even before the war, that I'd become a sniper if the war started because it's the specialization that best suits my abilities. I've always been a good shot, I'm patient and persevering, and I regard this job simply as a job, without any emotion—there's emotion when you listen to good music, watch a film or read a book, but not when you're shooting at the enemy.

At the time, I didn't suffer at all from having to fight. My husband, with whom I had gone to war, and other wonderful fighters were always by my side. Right from the start, we were mentally prepared for war, ruin, and loss, and we knew that this war was a fact, that it had its own internal logic, and that it was something inevitable, because imperial Russia would never voluntarily stop its attempts to annex Ukraine, and that we could only repel it by force.

Of course, things happened to me during the war. Once, I was thrown out of a building by an explosion and suffered a concussion and torn ligaments in my foot. Another time, a tracer bullet hit me in the face and the phosphorus burn scar was still visible on my cheek long afterwards. But as time goes by, we remember these moments with a laugh.

At the end of 2017, I returned to Kyiv, took an officer's course at the military academy, obtained the rank of second lieutenant and special training as an artillery soldier, and signed a contract with the Ukrainian armed forces. I didn't consciously choose artillery and never really liked it—but that year, no other specialization was on offer. Then, from 2018 to 2020, I served as an artillery officer in the Navy. I passed an extremely difficult obstacle course and earned the right to wear the Navy beret, the color of ocean waves. I also received a high distinction from the State: the Order of Courage, Third Class.

At the end of 2020, I left the army for health reasons. I had no intention of returning to the army either, I wanted to look after my health and my family. In mid-2021, my husband was also discharged. We spent a short vacation at the seaside, and then I became seriously ill again and underwent treatment; that was when the Russian invasion began.

I didn't want to go back. Neither to the army nor to the front. I was and still am a pacifist and a civilian at heart. To be honest, I'm finding it harder and harder, especially physically, as we're not getting any younger. But a person with combat experience has no moral right to stay away from combat in times like these. My husband and I returned to the army on the same day. Now I'm a deputy company commander, dealing with organizational matters and not firing directly at the enemy. This condition doesn't satisfy me, however, and I'm in the process of changing units, where I'll be fighting in the field again, alongside my comrades with whom I've been at the front since 2014.

Unlike most of my compatriots, I don't feel any hatred towards the Russians, even though I'm perfectly aware of all their crimes and receive news of the deaths of close acquaintances almost every day. War is war. It's us or them, and a hatred that burns from within wouldn't help me at the front. For me, taking part in combat is not about revenge, but about my duty as a soldier to defend my country. After our victory, if I survive, I'll certainly write a sequel to my book. I hope it will be published in a free European country that saved civilization from the savage Eastern hordes.

By Mariana Motrunych

Date of birth: May 30, 1991
From: Skole, L'viv Oblast
Profession: Communications manager, journalist, researcher
In Kyiv at the start if the invasion. Since February 2022, she has been going back and forth between Kyiv and Skole for professional reasons.

July 30, 2022

The war surprised me in Kyiv. I woke up to a phone call at 5:20 in the morning. My best friend, who lives near Boryspil International Airport, said: "The war has started. There are violent explosions here."

I got out of bed and approached the window. The street was already crowded. A family was hurrying to put blankets and suitcases in the trunk of their car. Everyone on the street was in a hurry. This was no ordinary morning in Kyiv. You could feel that something terrible had happened.

I listened and heard no explosions, even though I was only twenty kilometers from Boryspil airport. I turned on the TV, but there was no explanation. Suddenly, I ducked down because of a very violent noise. It sounded as if something had exploded right above my house. Alerted, I left the house ten minutes later in a hurry. I was afraid the Russians would blow up the bridges and dams and flood the left bank of Kyiv, where I live with millions of other people.

For almost a month, I'd already had a red can of gasoline in the trunk of my car. This reassured me. I always kept my documents in a separate folder, and my personal belongings were already in a suitcase I'd packed a few hours before the full-scale invasion.

I took along a pot of blooming flowers that I'd received as a gift the day before. I watered the other plants and left them sadly in the apartment. I didn't forget to take out the garbage either, to avoid an ecological disaster in the kitchen, and I took the stairs instead of the elevator.

Yes, I was prepared for the evacuation. Everything had prepared me for it, from communiqués from the international community to meetings at work. And after burning documents and removing the tricolor flag from the Russian embassies in Kyiv, L'viv, and Odesa, there was no doubt in my mind. It was the 23rd, and at dawn the next day, the Russian army invaded our country. In general, I had no doubt that Russia would one day attack Ukraine. Perhaps because of my origins and the environment in which I grew up, I never considered the Russian government to be friendly.

My friend was already waiting for me in the parking lot. His mother, who lived not far from me, categorically refused to accompany me, as did my friend who had woken me up in the morning. So the two of us set off, following a long-planned itinerary.

As I was driving, I could control my emotions fairly well by concentrating on the road. I was very angry and horrified. Even though I was prepared for the possibility of an evacuation at any moment, I had great difficulty managing my emotions and adapting to the new reality. I couldn't understand why I had to leave my home, why I had to give up my life in Kyiv because of Russia. I couldn't plan anything, I didn't know what tomorrow would bring, or even if there would be a tomorrow. Never in my life had I felt so much hatred, anger, and uncertainty at the same time. Military vehicles were driving in the opposite lane, and cars were stopping to let them pass. Fear and despair were evident on the soldiers' faces. I felt terribly sorry for each and every one of them. They were on their way to the place from which everyone else was fleeing.

There were lots of people on the road. There were long queues at petrol stations, stores and cash machines. People even took the back roads to avoid the major traffic jams on the main roads. It's hard to imagine what it was like at railway stations. Later, acquaintances told me that people would even leave their suitcases on the platform to get on the train. With babies, with the elderly, with pets. They would stay upright just to escape the missile attacks.

Two or three hours later, while I was still at the wheel, a video appeared on the Internet showing Russian armored vehicles crossing the Senkivka border crossing, in the Chernihiv region, on their way to Ukraine. It was very strange. I remembered that a few years earlier, I had worked with a cameraman on this same crossing. At the time, I was preparing a video report on the embezzlement of funds intended for the construction of the "wall" that was supposed to protect Ukraine from Russia. The question on my mind was why they had been able to enter our country so easily. Did our border guards resist? How, in 2022, can tanks enter a foreign country? What had happened?

There were reports of rocket fire and the first casualties. There was talk of casualties in the north and south. I was shocked to hear that the enemy army had taken Snake Island. It was said that the Russians had attacked the island, resulting in the loss of contact with the Ukrainian border guards, who had probably all been killed. It was so frightening. For a moment, it seemed that we wouldn't be able to defend ourselves, that part of Ukraine would be destroyed and conquered by the Russian occupiers. These thoughts made my blood run cold.

When night fell, I saw lights in the sky. They were rockets. I'll never forget that day, that night, and the nights that followed. The feeling of total injustice overwhelmed me. I wanted to turn around and go back to Kyiv because that's where my home is. But I couldn't, my mother was waiting for me in my hometown in Podkarpackie.

When we arrived at my mother's house around noon the next day, my aunt was there. She told us that her son had returned from abroad to defend Ukraine against the invaders, even though he had never held a gun. A few days later, we learned that my cousin from Lviv had also joined the Ukrainian armed forces. He's a scientist with no military experience. And there are thousands of people like that in our army. In this war, all those who consider themselves Ukrainians

must defend their country. Some with weapons, some with money, some through voluntary initiatives, or simply by doing their daily work properly.

Before Easter, I went to the cemetery where my late father lies. And there, I was surprised by a terrible feeling. I was happy that he was no longer a witness to this large-scale war. My father was always committed to Ukraine and its pro-European orientation. He actively participated in protests and rallies that defended democratic values, notably the Orange Revolution and the Revolution of Dignity. He was deeply concerned by the temporary occupation of Crimea and the eastern regions of Ukraine. He feared that the war would spread to the whole of Ukraine. And it did.

The atrocities that came to light after the Russians withdrew from the Kyiv and Chernihiv regions are indescribable and beyond imagination. How can anyone torture people, civilians? They're not guilty of anything. Why is there so much cruelty in the Russian army and such a need to feast on the suffering of others? I can't understand it. I simply can't understand how anyone can revel in human suffering, in making others suffer and watching them die slowly. Countless women, men, and children were raped, and thousands of houses and cars were riddled with bullets. Is this their "special operation"? Even in war, there must be rules. But for the Russians, absolutely any method of humiliation and destruction is acceptable, without exception. If I had a choice, I'd probably rather die than be captured by them. It's just too horrible.

I also have acquaintances who are now in captivity. They defended Mariupol. But I don't know if they're all still alive. I haven't had contact with anyone for over a month. I have no idea what's going on over there, what these people are thinking and feeling if they even exist. I can only pray that they have the strength to survive their captivity and hold out until their release.

The brutal war crimes are not committed by Putin himself but by ordinary soldiers and their commanders. For what purpose? Who is this enemy? Before this war, I distrusted the Russian leadership; after this full-scale invasion, I hate every Russian. All those who support this so-called military operation, who believe the propaganda, who are incapable of reflection and analysis. I wish them to hear at least once at home the terrible sound of the air raid siren and to tremble at the explosions.

It seems that nothing could be more terrible than what has come to light since the withdrawal of Russian troops from northern Ukraine, but we all know only too well that it can be even more terrible, for it is the physical extermination of Ukrainians; genocide. The Russian army proves this every time it drops bombs on the Kramatorsk railway station, on a shopping mall in Krementchuk, or destroys the center of Vinnytsia with missiles, killing thousands of innocent

Ukrainians. And what does the Russian propaganda say? That it defends Russian speakers? This is simply incredible hypocrisy. It is precisely in the Russian-speaking part of Ukraine that the Russian army is leaving scorched earth and ashes in its wake.

It was precisely this part of Ukraine that suffered most from the Holodomor organized by the Soviet regime in 1932-1933. According to various sources, between four and ten million people died of starvation. You have to imagine how many people died. They are mountains of corpses. This was at a time when Ukrainian fields were producing tons of grain. Today, in 2022, the inhabitants of Mariupol, Izyum, and many other Ukrainian towns and villages blocked by the Russians are dying just as horribly of hunger. This is madness. The Russians are once again stealing and selling our grain, passing it off as their own. They are burning the new harvest in the fields, without skimping on ammunition.

I think of my grandmother, who lived through the Second World War. As a child, she told me that when enemy troops invaded the village, her family went up into the mountains to save themselves, taking what they could with them. They were afraid of two armies: the fascist army and the Soviet army. My grandmother, however, was more positive about the Germans, saying that they were more humane and didn't take everything from people, just some of it. She added that everyone was very happy that the war was over. They hoped the horror would finally be over.

But even after the war, life didn't get any more colorful. Even Podkarpackie suffered the full brunt of Soviet rule, insurrection, prisons, deportations, financial injustice, lack of goods, and a total ban on the Church and all things Ukrainian. The Soviet government tried to make society anonymous and uniform. But it failed.

I'm as old as Ukrainian independence. I was born in 1991. My childhood coincided with the "terrible 90s," as they are often called. At the time, salaries weren't paid and there was a shortage of goods and food. The young state was trying to rebuild its economy. It was a difficult time financially, but the situation was improving year by year.

When the Revolution of Dignity began, I was a master's student. In November 2013, the first actions and demonstrations took place against the Ukrainian government's abandonment of the path to European integration enshrined in law.

After classes, many students went to the Maidan. There were mass gatherings, despite the cold and the risk of bloody repression. In the end, many people died in the clashes, ordinary civilians defending democratic values. Then President Yanukovych fled the country and Russian troops began to dismember our country.

In 2014, Russia brazenly annexed Crimea and launched its combat operations in the Donets'k and Luhansk regions. It legitimized this invasion with a pseudo-referendum. It is appalling hypocrisy to use such a democratic mechanism. In the end, the whole of Russia is shackled by propaganda and lies. Millions of people are brainwashed. No wonder they love the letter Z so much today.

It was against the backdrop of the political changes and bloody war in eastern Ukraine that I started working in investigative journalism. In fact, I threw myself into it headlong. I'd just finished studying history, so I was learning a new trade from scratch. From analytical work to shooting videos and writing scripts. It all fascinated me.

I wanted to be part of the changes, to make my contribution to the development of a democratic society. In this context, corruption was one of the main problems, even among the country's leaders. Most of my reports dealt with corruption. I was often asked if I wasn't afraid of my revelations. This question surprised me because, in our country, you can say anything out loud. Unlike Russia and Belarus, freedom still exists here, including freedom of speech. In any case, I've never encountered censorship anywhere.

However, investigative journalism is a very demanding job, which requires a lot of effort, costs a lot of money, and takes a lot of energy. Finally, in 2020, in the midst of the pandemic, I decided to change my profession. I started working at the National Anti-Corruption Agency. It was a very interesting experience, as I was discovering what it was like to work in the civil service. I was now sitting in the shoes of those whose activities I had critically observed as a journalist not long before. I saw how the public service was being transformed, albeit slowly and with great difficulty, but for the better. Bureaucracy and monotonous work are not for me, however, and so I resigned after a year to take a little trip at the end of the summer.

It was probably the first time I'd gone on vacation without my laptop, which I'd probably never parted with. It was a wonderful trip. I felt a certain lightness, even if I had no idea what I was going to do next. Without hurrying, I drove to the south of Ukraine, along the Azov Sea, and admired the beauty of nature. Fields of wheat as far as the eye could see, sunflowers, Kherson watermelons and melons, fragrant tomatoes. As I write these lines, I feel as if I'm back in time to last year's visit to southern Ukraine.

I lived in the village of Shchaslyvtse, in the Kherson region. It's located on the Arabat isthmus. It's a beautiful place. On one side, the warm Azov Sea, on the other, a salt lake where you can lie down. Not far away, is another pink, salty lake called Lemur Lake. Boat trips on the Syvash, where you can spend hours watching different species of birds.

Tourists came from all over the country. I could see this by looking at the cars' number plates, as the first two letters of our number plates designate a region of Ukraine. I didn't notice any pro-Russian atmosphere. The only thing I remember was Russian music on the beach. Certainly not very pleasant sounds.

This year, I was planning to travel to the Kherson region with my mother. On the way, we wanted to visit family members. They were forcibly relocated there as part of the "exchange of state territories" following an agreement between the USSR and Poland in the 1950s. As a result, over three hundred thousand representatives of the Boyko ethnic group found themselves in the south and east of Ukraine. From being mountain people, they became steppe dwellers. I think our project will only be postponed for a year. Very soon, Ukraine will re-establish its constitutional borders.

I'm very sad that the Kherson region has been occupied since the first days of the large-scale invasion. I'm afraid for the people who are still there. They are in constant danger. Everything they have acquired over the years and generations is being shamelessly taken from them. What's more, the Russians are kidnapping people en masse, humiliating them, torturing them, and some are simply murdering them. Living conditions under occupation are unbearable. People are forced to flee, to walk across fields under a blazing sun to reach free Ukraine. The expression "free Ukraine" now has a profound meaning. I care deeply about every corner of Ukraine, and every person who has to suffer from the invader.

I remember at university, we thought that the Revolution of Dignity had taken place because the older generation had failed to build a strong, truly free, and independent state. What's more, we wouldn't have won our independence in blood; it would have been given to us too easily. Today, the survival of our state has been won at the cost of the blood of thousands of civilians and thousands of soldiers, paramedics, ambulance drivers, railway workers, and volunteers. And ultimately, by all of us involved in this war. It is won at the cost of blood, tears, and great suffering. I believe we will defeat our enemy, the Russian Federation.

It was this country that for years conducted its propaganda here, even in the days of independent Ukraine. Russian culture was seen as greater, Russian pop as better, and the Russian language as more prestigious; everything Russian was considered good. Everything Ukrainian, on the other hand, was considered rustic and simplistic. Unfortunately, even after the start of the war in 2014, "Russian" was tolerated.

I hope it never happens again. After all, despite centuries of oppression, Ukrainian culture has survived, preserving its diversity and identity. Ukrainian is Ukraine's only official language, spoken by millions of Ukrainians. And there are enough people who would never be ashamed of their culture and origins, and who remain steadfast in their position.

Even when I was working in entirely Russian-speaking teams, I spoke Ukrainian. I never thought that my language should give way to another in Ukraine. I've lived most of my adult life in Kyiv, and that opinion hasn't changed. I value my culture and my identity, and these are important values for me.

All human beings have the right to make their own decisions. This is the case in democratic societies. It's also the case with us. My mother and I took in our estranged parents from the Donbas after Russia invaded Ukraine. For two months, we heard Russian and Ukrainian spoken at home, but it didn't cause any conflict. We were aware that they came from a Russian-speaking environment and that their mentality was very close to that of the Russians. That's what happened throughout history. Despite this, they still chose Ukraine. And they fled the war in the Podkarpackie, not in the forests of Bryansk or elsewhere in Russia.

Until February 24, 2022, I had plans that could very well have come true. I felt happy. Today, I find it difficult to envisage the future, as it depends entirely on the situation in Ukraine. From now on, I live in constant worry for my family, friends, and acquaintances. I want Ukraine to win this bloody war as soon as possible. I want all those who have committed crimes here to be punished, even if I doubt that will happen. If nothing is done, unpunished evil will cause even more suffering, wherever it appears. I hope that the people of Russia will find the strength to raise their voices. That they will remember their human nature and historical origins and finally destroy this horrible empire. Of course, I would prefer it if we didn't have this neighbor at all and instead had a beautiful, endless ocean, but that's wishful thinking, of course.

My mother still doesn't understand why her Russian cousin hasn't called her once to ask how we're doing. She doesn't understand how such a thing can happen. After all, the missiles reached us. Russian propagandists had been gloating on TV for days about the bombing of the Beskydy tunnel and bridge. Her cousin must have realized this. Especially as she knows very well that it's close to home; she's been here quite often, especially when she was younger. Her father was originally from here and always visited his country right up to the end of his life. So what has happened to her? Maybe she was dancing for joy with those propagandists when they announced the success of the Russian missiles. Maybe she did, but we'll never know for sure. We are certain that we will have no further contact with our Russian relatives. We don't want to know them.

Not long ago, I was in Kyiv. I went to my favorite shopping center for a coffee and a roll. That's where my favorite café is. I was surprised to see how empty the place had become. In the windows of some stores, the winter collections were still on display. The down jackets and warm suits looked very strange in the middle of June. I don't know when things will get back to normal. Probably never. Everything will be different.

My dreams are very simple, almost childlike. I want to be able to build my life here. I want to be sure that my house won't be destroyed by a Russian missile, that nothing will explode, and that I won't have to move. That people won't die because of the war and that no one will mutilate them as is happening now. I want to be sure that all Ukrainians can live in safety, peace, and tranquility. And most importantly, at home. I dream of being able to enjoy every day and live my life in peace in a free Ukraine.

No date is yet known as to when Ukraine will win this war and under what circumstances. I don't know how we'll get through the winter and into next spring. I don't know if Belarus will go to war. I only know that after the war, it will take us a long time to rebuild everything and come back to ourselves. More than one generation will still have to deal with the consequences of this terrible attack.

I know that years from now, Ukrainians, Russians, and Belarusians will start talking to each other and achieve some kind of reconciliation, but I really hope I won't be around to see it. Most Russians live in a sphere of total propaganda. And it will stay that way for a long time. It will take several generations before a dialogue can begin.

Meanwhile, I am staying in Ukraine. Despite all the open doors to the civilized countries of the world, I want to stay at home, because it is the place that is dearest to me, my home. And my home is the whole of Ukraine.

[Author's note: Mariana continues her work in strategic communications and open source intelligence, focusing on countering disinformation and strengthening Ukraine's information resilience.]

By Iryna Novokreshchenova

Date of birth: July 4, 1969
From: Zelenodols'k, Dnipro region
Profession: English teacher. Her son, Sergey, studies at the Odesa Theological Seminary, and her husband, Sasha, works as an engineer at the Krivoy Rog Thermal Power Plant (close to Zelenodol's'k).
In Zelenodol's'k at the start of the invasion; fled to Berlin with her daughter Dasha on March 13, 2002.

July 31, 2022

I was born in southern Ukraine, in the village of Novodmitrovka, in the Kherson region. I grew up there and graduated from Novodmitrovka High School with a gold medal. My region has always been famous for its watermelons. Kherson watermelons have always been the sweetest and the biggest. The average weight of a watermelon was between eighteen and twenty-five kilos. Near the village of Osokorivka, there was even a monument dedicated to watermelons, called "Gifts from the Kherson Region." In Soviet times, the Kherson region was also known for its variety of delicious, crunchy vegetables, which were exported to other Soviet republics and European countries. The Kherson region is made up of immense golden wheat fields. My father worked as an agricultural machinery engineer at the state enterprise "Bolshevik Offensive" and, together with the company's employees, achieved record wheat yields of up to forty quintals per hectare. He was responsible for fertilizing crops, especially wheat.

What is the situation today? My home region, Kherson, is occupied. The wheat fields have been set on fire by missiles and the harvest will not be complete. We may be able to save some of it, and there won't be a food crisis.

The news of the start of a large-scale military operation—or, more simply, the outbreak of war—hit me like a bolt from the blue. No one would ever have believed it possible. And now my dear mother and brother are living under occupation in the Kherson region. They lack food, electricity, gas, and contact with the outside world. Sometimes they receive humanitarian aid, or other people or organizations support them. When there is no electricity, my mother cooks on the gas stove. When there is no gas, she cooks with the electric oven. When there is no gas or electricity, my mother has to cook in the courtyard on an oven she built herself from bricks. I am very sad and worried about my mother and brother because I haven't been able to reach them for a very long time. I haven't heard my mother's voice for five months, since the 10th. March 2022, exactly since the moment I left my country, my Ukraine, my hometown of Zelenodol's'k.

I still vividly remember March 10, 2022, two days after March 8. Such a difficult time for Ukraine coincided with International Women's Day. My husband gave me some beautiful pink orchids. I was delighted. By then, the war had been raging for two weeks. March 10 was a very cold day, with a lot of snow. I took a cab to Apostolovo station, passing through two territorial defense checkpoints.

That day, there were two evacuation trains from the town of Kryvyi Rih, both passing through Apostolovo station. The first train arrived at four in the morning and simply didn't stop because it was already packed. People were rushing west to L'viv, then on to Europe and beyond. The second train to L'viv stopped on the platform and women with children quickly boarded, all very cold from waiting so long for the train. My journey to L'viv took almost twenty hours. In the carriage, the lights were turned off, the curtains drawn to camouflage us, and all the cell phones were switched off. There were eight of us in a compartment that was actually designed for four people. We sat huddled together, no one saying a word. Everyone was tired after that day, and fear and doubt were tormenting our souls.

As the train continued on its way, we could hear alarm sirens and explosions in the distance. During the journey, I worried about whether I would get to L'viv safely and quickly, and what I was going to do next. On the platform at L'viv station, volunteers welcomed us. They gave us hot meals and offered to help the children. I tried to calm down a little. As I walked along the platform and entered the underpass, I saw a very long queue. I learned that this was the queue for the train from Przemyśl in Poland. I stood in line and was very anxious, as I was expecting a call from my daughter Dasha, who had left Kyiv for L'viv. It was here, in L'viv, that we were to meet. Many thanks to the volunteers. They were very helpful, with distributing tea, coffee, sandwiches, and sweets. Finally, a call from my daughter. She told me she had arrived in L'viv. We were desperate to meet up and go to Poland together. Thank God, we met two hours later. The volunteers helped us carry our suitcases and get on board. There was still a bit of a wait before departure, and I was asked to help the volunteers distribute food and water to those present. I gladly accepted. At last, the train started.

Before we left, our passports were stamped, which meant we were leaving the country. Dasha and I hugged each other and started to cry. The train to Przemyśl was packed with women and children, mothers with strollers and babies. There were no free seats, so we and many others stood for ten hours as the train slowly made its way to Poland.

Finally, the train arrived in Przemyśl. It was bitterly cold outside and we were desperate to warm up. Here, the volunteers looked after us as if we were their own children, as if we were dear relatives. They organized hot meals for children and adults, advised everyone, and answered every question we had. We took the five o'clock train to Katowice. For the first time after two days without sleep, we warmed up and got some sleep. We then set off again for Germany.

I have a friend in Berlin, Johannes Baur. He helped us a lot in the early days in Berlin. He is a very friendly and warm person. There are no words to describe the kindness, hospitality, and cordiality with which we were welcomed by the volunteers in Germany. They were very supportive and helpful. They even managed to provide us with a variety of meals for all the unfortunate refugees: hot dishes, delicious sandwiches, heavenly smelling bread rolls, and many other goodies. I hadn't seen such genuine kindness, warmth, and love in a long time.

The Germans impressed me deeply with their concern for the Ukrainians who had fled to Germany before the war.

We first spent a few days in the small town of Bad Doberan, near Rostock, not far from the Baltic Sea. It is a place of beautiful nature, fresh air, and friendly people. We would like to thank the family of Christine and Tobias Baur, who hosted us in their home and helped us overcome the stress and fatigue of the trip. We felt well cared for and safe in their comfortable home. Their wonderful children enchanted us with their piano and theatrical performances. Listening to the music, we forgot the war and found peace.

Later, we moved to Berlin, with another family. Here, too, we were welcomed with hospitality, warmth, and comfort. The couple and their little daughter welcomed us with kindness and love, helping us to overcome our depression, anxiety, doubt, despair, uncertainty, and fear of the future. I am grateful to them, and especially to their little daughter, who was like a ray of light in the darkness.

I would like to share with you an event from my life in Berlin that I will probably remember for the rest of my life. On a warm spring day in March, my new family and I went for a walk and arrived at the square in front of the Brandenburg Gate. I saw the Ukrainian flag and heard Ukrainian songs. We drew closer. I was calm and happy, but when I heard the song entitled "A Prayer for Ukraine," tears welled up in my eyes and I couldn't stop crying. The couple, my family, with whom I lived, hugged me on both sides and their little daughter wiped my tears away with a handkerchief. She was so little, not even a year old. How could she feel my pain and suffering? Then I calmed down a little and we continued our walk, but my thoughts were already far from Berlin. They were in Ukraine, with my mother, my son and my husband.

War is so terrible. War is the separation of loved ones, relatives, and friends for an indefinite period. War is the fate of people lost for eternity. War is loneliness, doubt, and fear. War is the impossibility of hugging one's children, husband, or parents. War means many dead and wounded. War is the tears of mothers, wives, and children. War is the line that separates life before and life after.

I hate war. I don't like people who want to fight, shoot, and kill other people. God created us here on earth to love each other, to help each other, to live in joy, love, and grace. I love my country, Ukraine, very much. I would like to live with my family in a peaceful, prosperous Ukraine, and lead a long and happy life.

[Author's note: Sergey is finishing his fourth year at university. Sasha is involved in the reconstruction of the Krivoy Rog plant, which was damaged by Russian troops. Her mother still lives in the Kherson region. Dasha has secured a job and has been able to adjust to life in Germany. Iryna is currently enrolled in a German course.]

By Mariia Lepokhina, aka Masha Syta

Date of birth: March 12, 1993
From: Odesa
Profession: Model and Youtuber
In Odesa at the start of the invasion; fled to Berlin on April 16, 2022. Her parents, grandparents and husband are in Odesa.

September 5, 2022

I was born in the beautiful sunny town of Odesa, but as a child I often went to Russia, to visit my maternal grandparents. They live in the village of Ashukino, near Moscow.

How I loved these trips! Sometimes I would stay all summer in Ashukino. There, I learned to ride a bike, helped Grandma draw water from the well, learned to tend the garden, chased chickens, drank samovar tea and ate homemade jam, enjoyed our outings to Moscow, and went to church with Grandma every Sunday. Grandpa drank a lot and slept noisily, but he was very kind. Grandma was always a bit hard on me. I was a bit afraid of her.

I grew up in a family where there was no distinction between "us" and "not us." I grew up believing that Ukraine and Russia were friendly neighbors. At least, that's what my paternal grandparents told me.

Of course, I took history classes and remember that our territory was constantly divided between the Russian Empire, Poland, and Turkey. Sometimes we rallied to Russia, sometimes we tried to break away. We were told at length about the Holodomor of 1932-1933, the Stalinist repressions, and the "shot Renaissance" (the repression of the Ukrainian-speaking intellectual elite in the 1920s and early 1930s in the Ukrainian Soviet Socialist Republic). But these terrible pages of history couldn't stop me from loving Russia and my grandparents.

It was exactly after February 24, 2022, that my love for Russia completely disappeared and my Russian family ceased to exist for me. I don't even know if we'll ever get in touch again. After that fateful date, I didn't receive a single message or phone call from them. After a month of war, I wrote to the son of my grandmother Mamie's son: "Hello, how are you?" He replied: "OK," and didn't ask me a single question. He didn't ask me if everyone in our family was alive and if we needed help. I was so angry that I vowed never to write or phone them again. They love watching Russian television, so I have no doubt which side they're on in this war.

During the night of February 23 to 24, my husband and I slept with earplugs and were not awakened by the explosions. For some reason, I got up before the alarm went off and immediately looked at my cell phone. When I saw the message on the family chat: "The war has started," I realized that this was the end of my happy life before. I have a great ability not to panic in stressful situations and to keep a cool head. It was only in the evening that I allowed myself to cry. In the meantime, I packed two emergency suitcases, ran out to stock up on groceries, and then my husband and I went to fill up on gas. There were already huge queues everywhere, and you could see the terror on people's faces. At home, my husband and I taped up the windows, took the mattress off the bed, and put it in the hallway. Away from the windows. That day, there were two attacks in my town. It was very frightening.

At first, I thought it was Putin's war. I have a lot of Russian followers on YouTube and I addressed them on my channel. I received a lot of messages saying that they were sorry and that they were against the war. But I also received many messages such as: "Yuck, politics. A cop-out." or "What have you been doing for the last eight years?" or "Did you get paid to make these videos?" I received some lovely death wishes for all Ukrainians on my Instagram account. This hurt me the most because I've always believed in humanity and I've always thought that there are far more good people than bad in the world.

The next six months were the most terrible. The most difficult decision of my life was whether to go somewhere safe or stay with my husband. Dima was adamantly against me staying, but I couldn't bring myself to leave. For a month and a half, I vacillated between the two. As my fear of sirens and bombings grew, I packed my suitcase. It was hard to say goodbye to Dima because, in six and a half years, we'd never been apart for more than ten days. Yes, we'd also traveled alone, but we always knew we'd see each other again soon. The hardest part was realizing that I wouldn't be coming back anytime soon.

Sometimes I still feel guilty about leaving my family and husband in a country at war. Sometimes, when I walk around Berlin in the evening after eleven o'clock, I feel sad and guilty because my husband can no longer walk around the city at night so carefree. At home, there's already an eleven o'clock curfew, so he's always home by ten. I'm particularly sad when my husband is sad and I can't help him. I worry most about him during the Ukrainian holidays, when the likelihood of missile attacks is particularly high. Despite everything, I try to go on living. And Dima supports me in every way. He encourages me to work, do sports, laugh, see friends, and look after my health. He's never reproached me or told me I had to come back.

Those six months were the worst, but also the most amazing of my life. Alongside the horrors of war, positive and magical things have been happening. I've never seen Ukrainians so united and strong. Never have I been so happy to see my friends and family. Never have we settled our finances so quickly. Never have I received so many warm messages and offers of help from my foreign friends. I've never seen Ukrainian flags and other Ukrainian symbols in Europe. I attended the Independence Day procession in Berlin, and it was magnificent. We sang Ukrainian songs and shouted over the loudspeakers, everyone wore beautiful embroidered Ukrainian blouses and carried flags or placards. We cried, embraced strangers, and felt like one big family. All my friends, who used

to wander around Odesa's trendy places like snobs, now smile broadly and hug me when they meet me.

Of course, we've all changed, and we'll never be the same. It's certain that Ukrainians will continue to hate Russians for generations to come. It is certain that Ukraine will continue to lose many young and wonderful people. It is certain that all Ukrainians will have deep scars in their hearts from now on. There will certainly be people who are mentally and physically broken. The country will certainly need a long time to recover from this shock. Yet we must go on living for the sake of our freedom and our future. And it's certain that the whole world knows our country by now, and that no one will doubt any longer that Ukrainians are a formidable and strong nation.

[Author's note: Masha is now a resident of Barcelona and has a baby boy.]

By Olha Boravlova

Date of birth: April 30, 1988
From: Dnepropetrovsk, renamed Dnipro after the collapse of the Soviet Union
Profession: Screenwriter, editor-in-chief of popular programs, consultant to Ukrainian musicians, publicist, producer, mother of three
At home in the village of Petropavlovskaya Borschagivka (Kyiv suburbs) at the start of the invasion; fled to Essen in Germany and returned to Ukraine at the end of June 2022

July 30, 2022

I'm aware that among the millions of stories of Ukrainians, the attention of the international community is focused above all on the stories of children who have lost their parents, of children who have been killed. These stories also break my heart. But we Ukrainians feel like we're on a reality show. The whole world is watching while we compete in a game of "who had the worst experience in this war." So I ask you always to bear in mind that every story, every destiny deserves a little attention. And if someone has suffered more than others in this war, that doesn't mean those others don't deserve compassion in their grief. I'm a person who never complains, who never asks for pity, and who also likes to sympathize and help others.

The war showed me that it's not Ukraine that needs Europe, but Europe that needs Ukraine . . . My story is motivating and special. It was so even before the war. I'm the kind of woman who has made it on her own.

I've always had to make tough decisions. My biography in a nutshell: my father was a sadistic alcoholic who nearly beat me to death; beat me to death; my mother was selfish and cold, she poisoned my life; poverty and hunger during the difficult years of perestroika; an abortion at nineteen at my mother's insistence; prostitution at nineteen; accustomed to high adrenalin levels because of my childhood, I developed a passion for base-jumping (jumping off buildings, cliffs and factories); investigative journalism (filming in cemeteries, murder investigations, exhumations); a daily life of madness; two failed marriages; birth of three daughters. The divorces were on my own initiative, as I longed for a healthy relationship. The last divorce took place a year before the war. I was left alone with three children. I had to provide for them and pay for the apartment and the private kindergarten. I'm a workaholic and have always worked hard. I love to work. I had just succeeded in building a happy life for myself and escaping a difficult past . . . Starting from nothing, I managed to establish myself, become an expert in my field, and set up my own business, a creative agency.

On February 24, I had my usual busy day ahead of me. I had to drop the twins off at the kindergarten, and then head to the TV studio for a live appearance as a production expert. Then I had to meet my next customer, as we were planning a major sale. Not to mention my various routines: sports, healthy eating, driving school (I was in the process of getting my driver's license so I could finally transport my children).

I woke up at five in the morning because a military friend called me . . . he told me that the war had started and that I had to get the children out immediately. What do you mean war? What war? I have to be on the air today, I have meetings... My four-year-old twins were sleeping so peacefully... How can there be a war when my children are sleeping so peacefully and everything seems to be business as usual... I listened out the window to hear noises... I remembered my grandmother's stories about the Second World War. In my imagination, electricity was supposed to be cut off during the war, Internet, telephone connections, bombs were supposed to fall everywhere... and I should have been under the bombs with my children, and I should have taken them to safety.... But none of that. The silence... I thought of my eldest daughter, who was staying with her father. What if the link had been broken, what if it really was war and we had no contact at all? Suddenly, I was paralyzed with fear. I started reading my friends' Instagram messages and stories. I still wasn't sure if I should cancel my appointments for the day...

The singer I work with told me that bombs were falling near her home and that she feared for her life... Videos with the sound of sirens started appearing in the *stories* of my acquaintances... We had never heard the sound of an air raid siren. Turn a video on on YouTube, and listen to this... I googled it myself, not knowing what it meant. But I didn't even have to look for long, because the sound was suddenly heard outside... Breaking the silence in the whole street... That penetrating siren sound, deafening, terrible, and fighter planes start flying over our house.

In fact, I'm not afraid of anything... I'm a pretty brave and combative woman. It used to be that other people were afraid of me. A friend of mine, a policeman, always told me that in difficult times, he thought of my courage, and that gave him strength. But in the face of war, everyone is powerless...

The worst part is the unknown.

I don't have a car... I've never been abroad... I had no money... Like everyone else in Ukraine, I had to make a decision that morning. While my children slept, I tried not to panic and to think. What if it was all an illusion, just a small conflict, and everything would calm down in a few days? I can't just drop everything and drag my children out into the cold winter.

What happens if we're bombed in an hour and I can't take the kids and we die?

What happens if the connection is interrupted and I can't reach my children's fathers?

I hadn't spoken to my mother in years, because of everything she'd put me through. Terrified, I finally called her to see if everything was all right... She was asleep and didn't yet know that the war had started... I woke up the children and tried to make their morning as normal as possible. I prepared everything we needed in case we had to leave.

I washed my hair to look good in the *stories*. I looked at my nails and saw with concern that my manicure was chipping and that I would have to do another one tomorrow. Where could I go with nails like that? These little things are the habits of a quiet life that we cling to because we're unable to grasp a new reality. Just yesterday morning, I was doing my nails and waxing my legs, intending to make love to my boyfriend. And today, it's all gone . . .

And then they started firing rockets at residential houses . . . where my friends and acquaintances live . . . I finally understood that this was a real war and that we could get killed here. My children slept standing up for three days. We left for the border without money or a plan.

Maybe I've been luckier than others in some respects. I have a lot of good contacts, and journalism has given me skills that are useful for survival. But it's all for nothing if panic sets in and you're on your own.

You should know that Ukraine is a very large country. Many people stayed in the western part of the country, near the border. My fear was so great that I walked two kilometers with the children to the border and crossed it at night in a terrible stampede. Into a total unknown. Fortunately, there were already volunteers at all the borders. In Romania, we were assigned a family who took us in. I crossed the border twice. The second time, I went to pick up my eldest daughter; my husband didn't want to let her go at first.

Then I decided to go to Germany to stay with friends. We spent three months there. First, we lived in a hotel, then we got an apartment. Finally, I returned to Ukraine. In Germany, there were a lot of complications and conflicts.

It's July and we're in Ukraine. We're afraid of being killed by a missile. We're afraid Kyiv will be attacked again. We're afraid of an atomic bomb being dropped or a nuclear power plant exploding . . . These power plants operate in Ukraine . . . We're afraid that dams will be destroyed and the whole country flooded . . . Did you know that the depths of the Black Sea contain sulfurous water? At the beginning of the last century, it was on fire . . . Waves of fire scorched the coast and the people who lived there . . . If the conditions are right, the Black Sea can also be dynamited. It's a unique water on our planet—I've interviewed ecologists, so I know. The Russian army is poisoning our air, our water, our environment. Ours—not just Ukraine's, but the whole planet's . . . And it affects everyone. They're killing our bees . . . if you know what I mean. With the money from the war, Russia could have enriched its cities and its people . . . But they're spending that money to kill the citizens of another country. Missiles kill people here every day. My children used to be in Irpin all the time because that's where their father lives. He barely escaped, but the whole world knows what happened in Irpin . . . Today, my children are back in Irpin. Over there, the houses are destroyed, and the playgrounds are riddled with bullets. And my children play on the playgrounds destroyed by the war. I'm afraid they'll accidentally step on a mine or mistake a bomb for a toy.

My decisions. Why did we come back? In Germany, it was difficult for me psychologically. I didn't get on with my mother. This is a problem for many Ukrainian women. We were no longer living with our parents, and suddenly we had to do it all over again. There were other reasons. There was no kindergarten space for my daughters in Germany. It's a conservative country and very slow. There's no business like a creative agency there and no possibility of opening one, there's pressure and mobbing from Russians and Ukrainians who left there years ago. And much, much more. Children are separated from their fathers. It's terrible. Everyone is silent about the refugees' problems. The displaced people have so many problems that many are on the verge of suicide.

We returned to Ukraine in a private chauffeur's car, for five hundred euros. In fact, I just wanted to settle a few business matters. Then I could go back to Germany. But this adventure completely destroyed me. When we arrived in Ukraine, the driver started complaining that my daughters were going to the toilet too often . . . and demanded that I give them tablets so they wouldn't get sick . . . He said he wouldn't let the girls go to the bathroom anymore . . . He was a Ukrainian who had been in Germany for twenty years . . . It went so far that he threw our stuff in the middle of the road and threatened to leave us into the woods. By this time, my phone battery was almost empty. I just had time to call the police. In the end, he was forced to take us home. And the police warned him that he would be checked at every checkpoint and that if anything happened to us, the police would have his details. Put yourself in my shoes . . . what it felt like to drive another four hundred kilometers with this madman. And anyway, I was afraid to cross Ukraine, because, in the end, I couldn't see clearly where it was dangerous (which territory was being shot at, where there were threats of missile attacks, etc.). How could I take my children to a country where there was war? I didn't want to take them with me, but the Neu-Isenburg office wouldn't let me leave them in Germany, so I had no choice. Many people have suffered from this driver, who transports parcels from Ukraine to Germany and from Germany to Ukraine. Many told me later how insolent he had been with them. In his car, I feared for my children's lives and for my own. This adventure simply made me lose my mind.

I'm telling you, we underestimated our country. We didn't know ourselves how cool we were. Make up your own mind:

- Our boxers Klitschko and Usyk are world champions.
- Tania Muñoz directs music videos for global stars such as Katy Perry, Lil Nas X, and Cardi B. In 2021, she won the US *MTV Video Music Awards* for Best Direction and Best Video.

- The athlete Serhiy Bubka holds thirty-five world records!
- The Antonov 225 is the world's largest and most powerful aircraft and has set 240 world records.
- The helicopter's inventor is Ukrainian aircraft designer Igor Sikorsky, who emigrated to the USA.
- Ukrainian Serhiy Korolev is a rocket and space technology designer and the founder of cosmonautics.
- Yosyp Tymchenko was the man who, two years before the Lumière brothers' discovery, developed the world's first kinetograph with physicist Mykola Lyubymov. In 1893, two films shot with the first kinetograph were shown in Ukraine. However, due to state quarrels at the time, his device was not patented.
- Mykola Pyrogov, the founder of military field surgery, introduced the use of anesthesia during surgery and was the first in the history of world medicine to use a plaster cast.
- Yuriy Voronoi performed the world's first kidney transplant.
- Ukrainian Yegor Anchyshkin, 26, taught a computer to recognize human faces. The internet giant Google bought the technology.
- Leonard Kleinrock, one of the fathers of the Internet who emigrated to the USA, is also Ukrainian.
- In 1949, Kharkiv-born costume designer Varvara Karinska won an Oscar. Karinska was enthusiastic about working with Marlene Dietrich, Vivien Leigh, and Ingrid Bergman.
- Ukrainian singer Kvitka Tsysyk sang the soundtrack to the film *You Are the Light of My Life*. The song so moved film academics that it won an Oscar in 1978.
- In 1992, one of Hollywood's most famous actors, Ukrainian Jack Palance, took to the stage to receive his first statuette.
- In 1988, a Ukrainian actor popular in Hollywood, Eugene Mamut, received a technical award from the Academy. For a quarter of a century in Hollywood, this Kharkiv native has been involved in creating special effects for the world's most lucrative films, from *Dirty Dancing* to the legendary *Matrix*. However, Eugene received the coveted statuette for the film *Predator*.

For me, it became clear that Ukraine is a very progressive country, and that there is no such thing in Europe as what we have in Ukraine: delicious coffee, an active life, good service in the service sector, a high-level beauty industry, good television and *show business*, and complete digitization. And above all, FREEDOM. No, Germany is not a free country. But Ukraine is a free country.

Why do we Ukrainians feel that Germany is not a free country? Despite our gratitude for the help it gives to refugees, I'd just like to try and explain:

- Rules. European society is used to rules, they are the norm in people's lives. In Ukraine, there have never been any rules since the beginning of its existence, so people have gotten used to looking for other ways to solve their problems. This may sound frightening, but it gives more freedom and possibilities. From my point of view, a situation where everyone is equal is a motivation for laziness. You don't have to work, and you can live off state benefits . . . That's not the case in Ukraine, and that's why we're motivated to find ideas, and solutions and adapt. We're fast, perceptive, and active. In Germany, everything is slow and you always have to wait for something.
- In Germany, advertising and service are not well developed. Companies don't compete for customers. One company doesn't try to be better than another. And it shows. That's why you find tasteless coffees in cafés, a limited number of drinks on the menu, and little quality in the beauty sector. In Ukraine, everyone strives to have the chicest café, the best coffee, the most original layout, and the most active advertising, and that means freedom of action. In Germany, you don't have to do anything for your business. It simply exists. It is what it is.
- Why can't we film in public places? We're in the age of digitization. Video is very common. On the contrary, we should be teaching people how to use it, not restricting it. Encourage them, emancipate them. Do not restrict them.
- Why can't a street musician just stand in the street and sing a song? It's part of the culture . . . How can this be considered an infringement of law and order?

It's a bit strange to see things like that, isn't it? Whereas in Germany, LGBTQIA+ and transgender people are respected and most people in Ukraine still have a negative attitude towards them, we still consider Germany not to be free. It's a paradox. There's simply a difference between our cultures and lifestyles. It would be nice if we could learn from Germany's positive qualities. But Germany can also learn a lot from Ukraine. For example, freedom.

And I want freedom for myself and my children.

What is our life like today? Survival. Always planning for tomorrow, no long-term plans, thinking about evacuating again if necessary. I'm afraid for the people and feel sorry for them. Why did our neighbors come here to kill us? Why is the whole world watching like a reality show and not stopping this

war? I know why because I can analyze it. Propaganda technologies are also part of my job. That's why I can untangle this skein of propaganda and find the beginning. And at the beginning of this imbroglio, there are some completely unexpected things.

I've started writing a book on promotion, on advertising strategies, with the provocative title *The Toilet Book*. Among other things, it's about how to promote Ukraine as a unique country. It's also about mentality, financial and sexual education, our abilities, and weaknesses.

I'll do it while I'm still alive.

I love living so much. Now I just want to live, and I want my girls to live. And I want those horrible women to live, bickering with me in the store line. Because there's nothing worse than murder . . . I never expected such hell on earth.

And you know what, I invite you all to come and visit Ukraine. Maybe not now, but when the war is over. Extreme fans can of course follow the example of Angelina Jolie and other courageous celebrities who visited us during the war. Yes, you won't like everything the first time around—you'll have to delve a little deeper into the essence of this country and its people. I'm ready to accompany you on this journey. And I'm also willing to put you up, just as you put me up. And you Germans can always count on my help, on my hospitality. You'll find me on Instagram. I'll show you Ukraine. I'll take you out for coffee, I'll show you our beauty industry. I'll be happy to reveal the secrets of our television, *show business*, and media. I'll be happy to show you what we call freedom. We can share our experiences. I look forward to meeting you with an open heart.

[Author's note: Olha got married a year ago and has just given birth to her fourth child. The father of Olha's eldest daughter has been mobilized and is fighting at the front.]

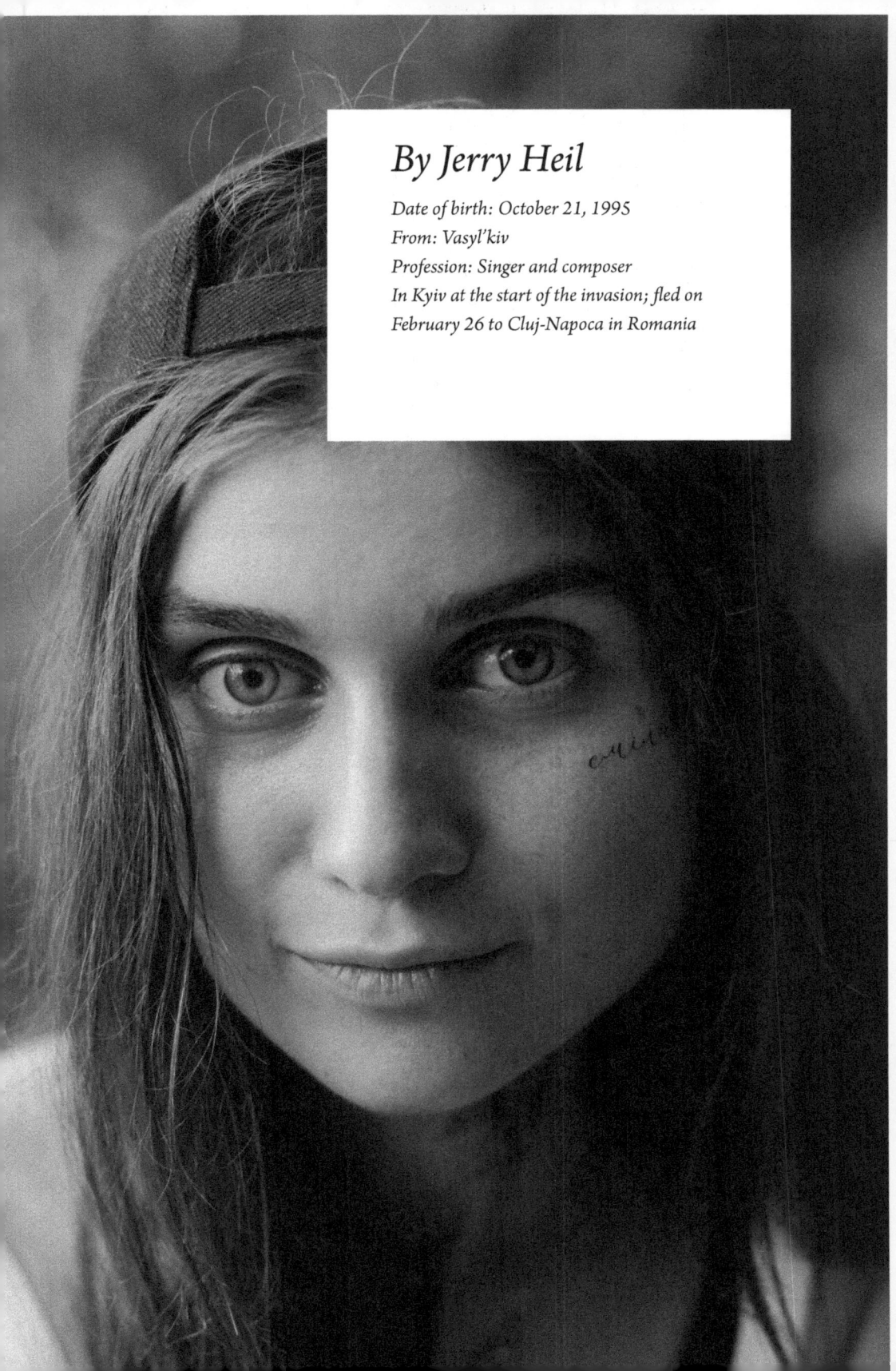

By Jerry Heil

Date of birth: October 21, 1995
From: Vasyl'kiv
Profession: Singer and composer
In Kyiv at the start of the invasion; fled on February 26 to Cluj-Napoca in Romania

August 4, 2022

Hi! I hope you're safe reading this, that the war in Ukraine is over, that the Ukrainians have defended Europe's security and proved themselves to be a nation of brave, singing people forever, in spite of everything.

In the media world, my name is Jerry Heil, but my parents call me Yana. I'm a Ukrainian singer and songwriter, a Ukrainian refugee since February 25, and an activist working to ensure that Ukrainian music is heard in Europe since February 27.

A few days before the war, the air in Kyiv became heavy and tense. In the street, I heard some people talking about fleeing to the west of the country, while others spoke of those who had already left. Some nodded in understanding, others squinted with contempt. I called my parents, urging them to get passports: "Why haven't you got any yet?" I shouted just to wake them up. I didn't think there was really going to be a war. The day before the war, I was having a coffee at Idealist Café. The usual background music was playing, but the customers' voices covered it and blended into a uniform gray noise. In this sound was the foreboding of war. It was a sound you could even feel on your skin. And what's more, it was a gray day. The air felt frozen. It was as if people were exhaling fear instead of carbon dioxide, which ended up taking up all the oxygen space. I called my parents again. This time, I was really panicked.

"You said nothing would happen, darling!"

"You still have to be careful! But nothing's happening," I lied to myself and my parents.

I was sitting alone in the house I'd just rented in Vyshhorod, and news of the Russian army on the border leaked out of every crack.

FEBRUARY 24TH MORNING. I opened my eyes. Silence. Darkness. I looked at the clock. I still had a few hours before I had to get up, but I felt the same fear that I'd felt in the city centre and couldn't get back to sleep. As soon as I opened my eyes, it felt like a countdown had begun. For a minute. Three... two... one... BANG! What was that? Fireworks?

I opened the window. This time, I didn't just hear the explosion, I saw it. And again and again. The black sky lit up with incredible shades of pink and orange. BANG! BANG! I soon realized that the military installation the Russians had attacked was probably very close to my house, but I had nowhere else to go. I was alone in the house, I didn't have a car, and cab drivers don't like to go out that far. My fear turned into hysterical laughter. The first call came from my manager: "Yana, it's war. We're hanging in there, regrouping and we'll see." I started googling. According to Google, there was no war in Ukraine. I was afraid: if journalists don't write anything, what are people going to do? Where would they go? But journalists are only human. They too have to go somewhere.

"My daughter, it's war! We must do something! Come home, let's think it over together!" my mother could barely speak through fear and tears of despair. Under no circumstances was I to lose my temper!

A few hours later, my assistant Roksolana and her friend, who also had nowhere to go, were already at my place. With cab fares rising by the second, my brother set off from the other end of Kyiv, from my hometown Vasyl'kiv, and didn't arrive at my place until around midday because of all the traffic jams. Then we came back the same way. A French friend left Kyiv at the same time as us, and we agreed to meet on the way.

Around three or four in the afternoon, on the first day of the war, I was in my hometown. There I learned that none of my family intended to leave. Hours of attempts to convince them, accompanied by the sound of fighter planes in the sky, were in vain. My mother even asked me to stay, but I had already promised to take Roksolana and her friend to relatives in western Ukraine. Sasha, who was due to start working for me as a driver that very day, was due to arrive any minute, so we all wanted to head in the same direction now.

We're off . . . "Don't cry! You'll see, in five days everything will be finished," I promised my mother, swallowing my pain. A few hours later, my voice had disappeared. Towards morning, after all the traffic jams and queues at service stations, we were already in Chernivtsi: me, my brother, our driver Sacha (whose grandmother let us spend the night at her place and gave me a hand to heal my sore throat), the two girls and my French friend Joffrey, who we had managed to find on the way there. They all stayed in the West. Only two of them wanted to continue: Joffrey, who had nothing left to keep him in Ukraine, and me, who had come to the realization that I had to go into the unknown to do something useful.

By morning, I'd packed the essentials: the laptop and a sound card with the microphone. This would allow me to live my life in every sense of the word. And that's what happened. Now, I confess in my songs as I would to a priest in church or to a psychologist. With the outbreak of war, I finally understood what was driving me.

Ukrainians now all have the same mission. It's not just about "defeating the enemy." It's much more than that. It's about "giving freedom to Ukraine," which also means the freedom to spread Ukrainian culture beyond its borders. During the four months I had to stay in Europe, I asked myself every day: how come people here still don't know about Ukraine's impressive nature, sophisticated technology, cities, and people? Why is it that Spanish, Italian, Romanian, and

French music are part of contemporary international pop culture, but not Ukrainian music? When you listen to an Italian or French song, you can immediately tell which country it comes from! How is it, then, that Ukrainian folk music, which comprises over five hundred thousand songs, has not been heard for its entire existence? Because the country and its culture have been fighting for survival for so long.

Maybe that's why we have so many popular songs, because even now, after the start of the large-scale Russian invasion of Ukraine, Ukrainian artists are creating music of astonishing beauty and depth!

At the Romanian border, we learned that Joffrey's car had been fined and couldn't cross the border, so he set off again to sort it out, and I set off on foot to Romania, to a country where I knew no one and where no one was waiting for me on the other side of the border. I packed up my music gear, hugged Joffrey goodbye, fought back tears, and crossed the bridge. Romania welcomed me with wonderful, almost aggressive (in the best sense of the word!) hospitality. No sooner had I crossed the border than they were handing me tea, almost stuffing a croissant in my mouth, and giving me a free SIM card!

I was greeted by strangers (computer scientists) who introduced me to their family. They had written on Facebook that they could help. After a few hours' drive from the border, I was already in Cluj-Napoca. There, I spent a few days reading the news, and learned that the rashists had destroyed military buildings in my hometown, then bombed an oil depot and caused an ecological disaster. And a few days later, again! On the phone, my parents asked me to pray only. Regenerating my voice under such stress was difficult, to say the least. I finally decided to go to a demonstration to sing about Ukraine, over there in Romania. And if not with my voice, then with my soul!

And then a miracle happened, and the same a few months later in Brussels, when the same situation happened again with the stress and the voice. I was backstage, I knew people were waiting for me to go on stage, but I couldn't even speak out loud. But there's something magical about Ukrainian folk music! The group Go_A, playing modern interpretations of traditional folk songs, performed in front of me. Suddenly, listening to one of their songs, everyone spontaneously grabbed hands and started dancing! I burst into tears and everything became clear at that moment. That's the strength of our people! Our unity is not a slogan on TV! This unity is rooted in our genes and was passed down to us by our grandparents, who in turn received it from their grandparents! We're such a strong nation that we've not only managed to preserve traditions and put them into practice on feast days, we live every day according to the laws of our ancestors! The tears eased the tension in my throat and I realized that my voice

had returned! After that key moment (and a few others, like in Amsterdam, where a crowd of ten thousand locals and Ukrainians sang the song PUTIN, GO HOME with me), I realized that I could finally make Ukrainian music heard around the world!

Perhaps my feelings are better expressed in my songs than in this letter. Because the songs themselves are already tinged with emotion. As I said before, they are my confession, my safe place, my psychologist. But also my mouthpiece and a network that unites the world.

[Author's note: Jerry has since spent a year in Boston and returned to Kyiv, where she composed a song for the book called "Call me freedom." She was awarded third place at the Eurovision song contest in 2024].

By Ira Solomatina

Date of birth: July 03, 2012.
From: Slavutych
Position: Schoolgirl
In Slavutych at the start of the invasion; escaped with her mother on March 31, 2022 to Jever, Germany.

July 30, 2022

My name is Ira, I'm ten years old. I come from the town of Slavutych. Before the war, I practiced choreography and learned to play the domra. My favorite game is Minecraft, which I play a lot. In the future, I'd like to travel the world to research and study rare animals. I now live in Germany, but my hamster Odi stays at home in Ukraine. I'm very fond of him, and I've always liked to hold him in my hand and stroke him when I've come home.

I feel good in Germany, it's totally happy and safe here. You don't have to wake up at night and go down to the cellar when the siren sounds, and you can go out whenever you like. In Slavutych, I was scared at first because at night, all the windows shook and you could hear explosions. We had little food and the stores were closed, but people helped each other and shared their food. Then there was no electricity and my parents cooked food on the fire. And when the electricity came back on, we rejoiced as if it were a holiday.

I have absolutely no idea why Putin started the war. He's an idiot. I was always taught to solve all problems by talking, not by violence, to talk if you don't agree with something. I thought the Russians were a bit smarter and knew that war is bad and that it brings a lot of suffering to everyone. Why did they have to attack us? We were doing fine! I find this war absurd. I'm very disappointed with the Russians.

When our soldiers have driven out the Russians, will the war be over and can we go home? I miss my home, my friends, and my loved ones. When I go to bed, I imagine myself in my bed, at home, the better to fall asleep. After the war, Ukraine will be almost as it was before, destroyed houses will be rebuilt and Ukrainians will be even more united and love their Ukraine even more.

[Author's note: Ira now speaks fluent German, enjoys going to school, has friends in Germany and seems to be leading a happy life. But she refuses to talk about the war and doesn't like to remember it. Her mother says she is trying to erase this traumatic experience from her memory. Helplessly, she tries to encourage Ira to read books in Ukrainian, hoping that she will not completely lose herself in her new life.]

By Mariia Cherpak

Date of birth: October 18, 1994
From: Kharkiv
Profession: Marketing specialist and founder of a project dedicated to meditation and yoga
In Kyiv at the start of the invasion; escaped to Wrocław, Poland, on March 8, 2022 and now lives in Berlin, Germany

September 20, 2022

It may sound strange, but when I lived in Kyiv, I dreamed that my parents and I would live in the same city. That way, we could spend weekends together, have breakfast, go to the theater, or shopping together, and I could simply visit my family whenever I wanted. There's a reason they say you should dream more carefully. I've been thinking about this phrase a lot over the last six months. I now live in Berlin with my mother and my cat. In the city I had already planned to visit several times. The city I decided to go to in two minutes, without planning, at night while driving, somewhere in the middle of Poland on the freeway, on the fifth day of my trip out of Kyiv.

So I've been living here with my mother for six months now, and I'm glad I made the right decision. In that time, we've both managed to adapt our daily lives to each other. It's a bit like going back ten years to our apartment in Kharkiv. It was interesting to observe how certain patterns in the way my parents behaved with me have continued to this day as if I were thirteen again.

I've had to work hard on myself to adapt to living with someone who has a different schedule, different eating habits, and different habits altogether. But the hardest part was the role reversal in the relationship between parents and children. There's even a term for this: parentification. It's a process whereby children, for various reasons, take on the role of their elders and virtually become their own parents' parents. At one point, I became my mother's most important point of contact with the outside world. This involved communicating with everyone around us, endless paperwork, and organizing our new life. Over time, I realized that I couldn't take it anymore and that I had no energy left for my own development. So I concentrated more on myself and paid attention to my personal limits, which had changed a lot. I motivated my mother to get more involved. The fact that we take a German course together is very helpful. She's gradually starting to make contacts. But of course, I can't imagine how difficult it must be, especially for our parents who now live in another country, and not by choice. Many of them don't speak English and can't do anything on their own. That's why I'm aware of my responsibility and really want to give my mother the care she's given me all these years. We're very lucky to be able to listen to each other and live well together. My mother is my friend, and we share many interests and values. We go to museums, yoga classes, and cultural events. The most important thing is to remember that we're a family and that we need each other, now more than ever.

For the first few months, I found it very hard to allow myself to feel happy or appreciate anything. These feelings were banished and would remain so until we won this war. I remember my mother and I arrived in Poland and went to a shopping mall to buy slippers. We simply couldn't believe that life went on and that people were just shopping here. For half an hour, we sat on a bench in the middle of the mall, trying to get down the earth.

My most vivid memories of the phase during which my mind reacclimated to safety date back to the period from March to May. On the second day after our spontaneous arrival in Berlin, my mother and I went to museums, and we did this for about seven consecutive days. We felt such an inner emptiness and suffered such an overflow of negative feelings that we had an irrepressible urge to surround ourselves with beauty. We spent more than four or five hours in each museum contemplating the exhibits, interrupted only by the Ukrainian news. It was then that I realized why I felt so at home there. For me, the museum was like a time machine, where everything seems to stop, where the whole world pauses around you, where everything is silent, where visitors speak in low voices and move slowly between objects. In museums, it's always very quiet. It was one of the most memorable experiences: standing between ancient Egyptian sarcophagi and suppressing tears as you heard the news from home. Over time, the habit sets in. And that's perfectly normal. Otherwise, we simply couldn't survive. I've met many refugees who can't let go of what they left behind in Ukraine. They live completely in their thoughts of home and are constantly in a terrible emotional state that tortures their psyche. I understand how difficult it is, but you have to make a decision and feel what's best for you now: stay in Ukraine, leave completely, or leave and come back after six months. It's easier when you have a plan in mind.

It's a very painful experience to build a new life in safety when your country is at war, your loved ones are under fire and everything you hold dear is destroyed. One day, I realized that my psyche was leading a double life, shifting from one state to another according to the news arriving from my home country. You're sitting in German class, the sun is shining through the window, everyone is chatting, and then you turn to your pale mother who has just learned that a bomb has exploded near her old workplace. A close friend was there at the time. It turned out later that he was fine. And there have been countless moments like that. Or when you're waiting for a shell to hit your own house because all the neighboring houses have already been hit. At times like these, you simply can't function normally.

I remember the spring when we had just moved to Berlin and a kind of magic enveloped us. We met so many wonderful people with open hearts. One day, we were walking through a district of Berlin, discovering the city, when my mother noticed a beautiful flower store. She had worked as a florist in the Ukraine for twenty years and had a lot of professional experience. Naturally, she rushed to the window and looked around the store, then spontaneously asked me if I couldn't find out if there was a vacancy. I remember my surprise, as my mother is quite reserved when it comes to making contact with strangers, but here her eyes sparkled. We went in, approached an employee, and asked if it was possible

to work there without knowing the language. The store owner and staff were very friendly and open-minded people, who accepted my mother into their team, and now she's been doing what she loves for a few months now, integrating herself into German society. I'm very proud of her. This is one of the stories that taught me to knock on a closed door that might not be closed.

I have very mixed feelings about Germany. On the one hand, this country has welcomed Ukrainian refugees with open arms and given them considerable help, for which we are very grateful. On the other hand, the German government has pursued an indecisive policy on the question of how to support Ukraine with arms. It is also in no hurry to detach itself from Russian energy resources and has long worked closely with a terrorist state. When I moved here, I was surprised by the large number of Russians in the country and their strong integration into German society. But I was especially outraged by the fact that Russians could legally organize demonstrations in Berlin, during which they called for hatred against Ukrainians and used fascist symbols. How can such a thing be allowed when this country is waging an underhand, brutal war, murdering and torturing innocent people, including children, and the citizens of this country are openly applauding these atrocities on social media?

I feel Ukrainian and, more than ever in my life, I define myself strongly by my nationality. I feel like a person who comes from a very modern and developed country, with solid principles, a high standard of living, and incredibly talented and strong people. A country that is now defending a peaceful sky over the whole of Europe. I'm very grateful to Germany for welcoming us with open arms and giving us the support we needed to start a new life. Within the first few days, we met a German family in Berlin, who I can safely describe as our family's guardian angels.

I'm now going to say something that many Ukrainians wouldn't dare say in public, or even admit to themselves. I'm one of those whose life has been influenced in the best possible way by the war if you can call it that. For me, it was a kick in the ass—moving to another country, freeing my life from everything that had been holding me back and had long since stopped allowing me to be satisfied and evolve. If I look at myself today, as I was six months ago, I see a person with a lot of fears, prejudices, and limits in his head. I began to think less about what others might think of me and to do what made me happy: listening more to myself and my feelings and choosing more carefully the people, work, and everything else I let into my life. During the six months of my new life in Germany, I did a lot of inner work and was more in touch with myself.

[Author's note: After three years of war, Mariia has come to realize that technological leadership in defense is paramount. She is now volunteering to help identify promising European technology start-ups and connect them with various units of the Ukrainian Armed Forces for potential collaboration.]

By Sofiia Kropyvnytska

Date of birth: June 27, 2011
From: Kyiv
Position: Schoolgirl; wants to become a chef.
In Kyiv at the start of the invasion; escaped with her mother on March 1, 2022 to Leszno, Poland. They both returned to Kyiv on June 26, 2022.

July 26, 2022

On February 24, 2022, when the war started, I was at home with my parents in Kyiv. That same day, Mom and I went to visit Grandma, who lives near Kyiv. Now I'm back home in Kyiv.

My name is Sofiia, I was born in Kyiv and I live there.

Since the beginning of the war and still today, I'm afraid, because now nothing is like it was before the war, we don't plan anything and don't know what tomorrow will bring. I can't see my friends when I want or play outside when I want, because the sirens never stop wailing, and that's terrible. Every time I hear them, I'm sad and scared. Mom tries to be with me all the time, not to leave me alone.

A week after the war broke out, Mum and I went to Poland. Dad thought it was safer. Mom cried. I didn't know what was going to happen. With us went my aunt (Dad's sister) and her daughter. We drove for a very long time, first through Ukraine, then through Poland, I think for several days, before arriving late at night in Warsaw. We spent the night there, and the next morning went to a small town. Another day's drive and there we were, in an empty house in the middle of fields. There were five apartments in this house, all occupied by Ukrainian mothers and their children. After a while, I went with my cousin to a Polish school, where I studied for four or five months, and after classes, I did the homework for the Ukrainian school. At first, I had a very hard time at the Polish school because I didn't understand the language and I thought my classmates only talked about me. Mom was always looking for work. Sometimes she'd leave for work very early in the morning, while I was still asleep, and then my aunt would take us to school.

I was also very worried about my loved ones, about Dad and my friends who had stayed behind in Ukraine and had to hide in shelters all the time. I just wanted to come home, all the time, but Mom couldn't tell me when we were coming home.

Until the end of June, I went to school in Leszno (the town where we were in Poland), then we immediately returned to Ukraine. We were well received in the other country, but I was homesick. I still don't know if I'll be able to go back to my school in September, and probably nobody else does either, as my parents are worried and say it could be dangerous, as many schools have already been destroyed by the occupiers. But I'd love to go back to my school and see my friends again, whom I haven't seen for over five months.

My cousin's father, who was with us in Poland, is now in the army, protecting us. We're proud of him and hope that he will survive this war.

Besides, I really wish this damn war would end, that the occupiers would leave our country and never come back. Ever again. And I wish that Ukraine could become the best and most modern country, that all countries would want to be friends with us.

Later, I'd like to become a pastry chef and learn at cookery schools in Ukraine and France.

Before the war, I had a normal relationship with Russia, like with any other country, and I even spoke Russian sometimes, but now I've decided not to use that language anymore. I don't want to meet soldiers from the enemy army. I'm afraid of them.

The worst and most painful part was leaving Ukraine for an unknown country and ending up there indefinitely. My best memory is the moment we came home!

My biggest dream is for the war to end, and for all Ukrainians to be alive, healthy, and happy! I also dream of having a cat and a dog after the war.

By Yana Nakonechna

Date of birth: July 27, 1987
From: Kharkiv
Profession: Gynecologist-obstetrician
In Kharkiv at the start of the invasion; escaped with her mother to Münster, Germany

July 29, 2022

The day that changed my life.

February 23, 2022, was a perfectly normal day in my life. In the morning, at nine o'clock, I changed shifts as an intern at Kharkiv Maternity Ward. I went home with a feeling of satisfaction. When I get home, I always review my day in my head: what I have to do, and where I have to go next. This was the case this time. I decided to go to the gym. I hadn't worked out there for a long time, only since October. It was a new gym downtown. I especially liked the fact that it had a pool. I loved going there. But when I got home, I realized I'd forgotten my tablet at work, which had never happened to me in all those years, and I'd already been working at the hospital clinic for eight years. It would take me forty minutes to get back, but I didn't want to waste time. So I decided to ask my childhood friend, who had a car, for help. I called him and explained everything, and (hooray!) he wanted to pick up my tablet. I was thrilled. I quickly got my things ready to go to the gym. After the workout, I called my friend to give me the tablet. We met, had a cup of coffee, talked a bit about our years of study, and then went our separate ways. That was our last meeting, and I haven't seen him since, nor do I have any contact with him now.

When I got home, I watched a bit of television as usual. I cleaned the apartment and went to bed. But despite a twenty-four-hour shift, a workout, and no nap during the day, I couldn't fall asleep. I couldn't understand why I couldn't sleep. I usually sleep well after such a heavy workload, but this time, for some unknown reason, that wasn't the case. So I decided to spend some time on social media. I like to watch videos there, for motivation and personal development. The ones I like the most, I publish in my Instagram stories. What I posted a few hours before the war shocked me afterward, because one of the videos I posted on February 24, 2022, at 3:55 a.m. was like a prophecy: "Forgive me, old friend, I must wake you up . . ." At the time though, a few hours before the war started, I didn't pay much attention to this video, something about it just appealed to me, but in retrospect, it was a warning to me, perhaps from higher powers. I continued to surf the Internet for a while, then decided to go to bed. I closed my eyes and lay there in total silence, turning from side to side. It was impossible to fall asleep.

At 4:40 in the morning, I suddenly heard four muffled bangs, distant but loud. I got up, went to the window, looked outside, and everything was quiet as usual, but I had a bad feeling. I walked around the apartment and wanted to talk to someone, but who, it was five in the morning, and everyone was asleep . . . but I just wanted to talk. So I decided to call my friend who had picked up my tablet from work. I called him and said: "Sorry to bother you, but I can't sleep, I'm very agitated. Do you know anything new about the situation with Russia?" He told me I was worrying about nothing, that everything was fine, and that I should go back to bed. Still, I couldn't sleep. I turned on the TV and there was nothing interesting on either, just the usual. Around half past five, I noticed that there was a lot of traffic on the road leading out of Kharkiv. It was unusual at this early hour. For some inexplicable reason, I was worried and nervous. I got dressed and ready for the eight o'clock shift. At six o'clock, my friend and colleague called me and simply said: "Let's go, pack your bags." After that, everything was like a fog. I had noise in my ears, fear in my eyes, and only these phrases in my head: "It's not possible, it's not possible, we live in civilized times in a civilized country. What war? Is this a joke???" My heart is pounding like after a marathon. I run around the apartment not knowing what to do in a situation I couldn't have imagined in my worst nightmares. I call my friends, who are also my colleagues, and tell them, "Wake up, the war has started."

I then called my parents, who didn't live in Kharkiv but nearby, and asked them to put all the valuables in one place and to call me if they heard anything. Since January, I'd had two suitcases packed, just in case. One with documents and photo albums, the other with clothes. These suitcases were small. I always used them as hand luggage, so they couldn't hold much. As a conscientious person, I wanted to go to work with both suitcases. I went to the bus stop and waited for my bus. I waited for an hour, then another hour, but the bus didn't arrive. I called my colleagues and told them that unfortunately, I couldn't come to work. They told me not to worry, that they would replace me, and that I could stay home today. I went home, put my suitcases by the door, turned on the TV, and then officially learned that there was war in Ukraine. The city was in a panic, and I could see from the windows of my apartment that a general panic had broken out and people were leaving the city. I sat there for a long time, then decided to buy some food, just in case it ran out . . . So I went into the store across the street, where it was very busy and the shelves were emptying. I panicked and took everything with me, whether I needed it or not . . . When I got home, I turned on the TV again. I saw the terrible news and videos again. I thought maybe it was gunshots that had made so much noise this morning . . .

All day long I sat in front of the TV, even at night I didn't turn it off. I was lying down, dressed, and it was the second night in a row that I couldn't sleep. I was so tired that I ended up falling asleep for a few hours. I woke up to the sound of a passing tank. I jumped up, ran to the window, and saw a column of tanks entering the city—it was a horrible sight. After that, I couldn't sleep. To distract myself, I turned the television back on. Since the morning of February 25, I've been calling my parents and friends all the time, wanting to know if they're all right. Thank God, they're all alive and well. The television is on twenty-four hours a day. I sit at home all day, afraid to go out, and sometimes I hear gunshots in the distance. Tanks come and go, it's war. It is not a war movie, it is reality, the terrible reality in which we live! The whole day passed in fear, waiting for something to happen. Probably waiting for the next newscast to say: "That's it, it's over . . ." In the evening, as the day before, I lay in bed, dressed, with the TV on, ready to leave at any moment . . . But where to go? Where was I supposed to go? To an air-raid shelter? Were there any left at home? Of course not, who could have imagined that seventy-seven years after the end of the Second World War, which my grandmother, who is still alive and ninety-six, had told me about, I myself would have to live through a period of war?

At night, the explosions don't stop. I always fall asleep and wake up. I don't jump anymore when the tanks pass by, I just press the pillow tighter against my ears so I can't hear the noise. In the morning, I call everyone I know, and they're all still alive. Around noon, I get the idea of leaving Kharkiv to visit friends in Germany. I called all my friends and relatives and offered to flee the war with me. Unfortunately, no one was ready to give up everything they had worked so hard for, to leave their loved ones behind, to leave their apartment and their job to go somewhere . . . I called my mother and suggested it. After listening to me, she tried to reassure me and said we should talk about it the next day. I agreed. I then called my father to find out what he thought. He was against it and told me to come to their house.

The same day, not much time had passed, my mother called me back. She agreed. It was already around five o'clock, and she wanted to pack her bags and join me in Kharkiv. However, the question was how to get there: there were no buses, and it was too uncertain by car. She called every possible cab number and asked for a ride to Kharkiv. One cab driver agreed, but only for one thousand hryvnia (whereas the normal price of a bus ticket is around sixty hryvnia). I ran off to buy some food for the journey. On the way, I met someone I'd known for years but hadn't seen for a long time; he was wearing a military uniform and was on his way with another. We talked a bit. They were on their way to the military police station to sign up for territorial defense. Young men with wives and children going off to war to defend the country . . . I couldn't control myself and started to cry, he took me in his arms and tried to calm me down, but the tears just flowed, I didn't care how many people were there, we just stood there and said goodbye . . . We said goodbye, maybe forever.

A few hours later, my mother was already in Kharkiv, with a small bag containing clothes and documents. We called a cab and went to the station. I was shocked by the number of people there. There was a terrible noise, crying, shouting, and gunshots in the distance. We were at the door of a carriage, the train was due to leave for L'viv. We stayed there for about three hours, and it was still winter. My mother and I were cold, but we were still there, waiting. On the tracks, there were suitcases and clothes, abandoned animals walking around . . . As we waited, my strength began to fail and I could no longer feel my legs. Then the bolt slammed and the door opened. Hysteria, panic, a stampede. People rushed to the door in panic, disregarding children or the disabled, driven only by an animal instinct to survive in any circumstances, even if others had to die. My mother and I stood just inside the entrance. I hadn't expected such an influx and was very much afraid that we would simply be thrown onto the tracks. I turned around, my back to the entrance, one suitcase in my hand, the other in my mother's, who was also carrying her bag. When I turned around, I saw her eyes, which were full of fear and pain. I couldn't move, I was caught in a vice, I was looking at my mother and she was looking at me. I could see that she wanted to help me, but she just couldn't. In this desperate situation, I thought: "This is it, this is the end."

Then someone on the train helped me lift my suitcase and get on myself, I was stuck in the passage and the others couldn't move either. If I had fallen, I would have been trampled. That's when my suitcase was lifted onto the train and I was able to get on. I was shaking with fear and shock. My whole body was shaking.

I looked back at my mother and saw her being pushed from all sides, I tried to take her suitcase and help her somehow, but I had no strength left in my arms. We barely managed to get on the train and into a compartment. I was under a lot of stress and the tears were flowing. The compartment was completely packed. There were fifteen people in our compartment. I don't remember what time the train left. We rode all night without stopping until we reached Kyiv, huddled together. The windows were closed and we felt like we were suffocating. Only one window in the corridor opened occasionally, but not for long because the people lying on the floor were cold from the wind. I couldn't stop crying. I didn't know if I'd made the right decision to leave Ukraine and take my mother with me. Had I made a mistake? Maybe it would all be over tomorrow? And a host of other thoughts ran through my head . . .

I couldn't hold back my tears. They flowed freely. My mother was trying to calm me down and was probably crying herself. From time to time, I felt the urge to grab my things, get off and walk home! But this train had only one stop: L'viv. Before that, nobody got off or on. As we passed through other towns, I saw panicked people rushing to the trains and demanding that the doors be opened. They were trying to escape, trying to survive. In our car, the doors didn't open until L'viv. We traveled for about eighteen hours. We finally arrived in L'viv. When we got off, we breathed in the fresh air eagerly. How good it was to breathe fresh air . . . We arrived in the evening and wanted to find a place to spend the night, so I called every inn and guesthouse I could find, but everything was busy. We were stuck at the station in the evening in winter. We didn't know how to continue our journey, and we didn't know where to spend the night either. I called a relative of my friends in Germany who had gone to Lviv the same day, only by bus. She answered. We didn't know each other yet. She was also at the station and wanted to continue to the Polish border. We decided to go with her.

The driver asked each person for two thousand hryvnia for the journey, and we set off for Mostyska. It was already dark. We arrived at a school where we could spend the night for free. We checked in at the entrance and looked for a place to sleep. When we entered the gymnasium, we saw that everything was occupied. There were no mattresses, people were lying in the changing rooms next to each other, even with animals, a very peculiar sight. We asked to go to another room and arrived in a classroom where there were fewer people. We were also given mattresses and blankets. After making our beds, we were able to go into the dining room and drink hot tea. After such tiring days, it was nice to be able to sit and drink tea. After we'd sat and talked for a while, I realized that we'd already been on the road for thirty hours; it seemed like half an eternity. I finally lay down and fell asleep immediately, but unfortunately, I didn't have time to sleep for long. Cats were running around the room and rummaging through every pocket, but the worst was the snoring of the man next to me. He snored so much it was simply unbearable, and I lay there for about an hour hoping it would stop soon. Unfortunately, it didn't . . . Finally, I approached the man, woke him up, and asked him to turn on his side because I couldn't sleep through his snoring. The man quietly turned over and stopped snoring. So I too was able to sleep peacefully for a few hours.

The next morning, we woke up early and went to the bus stop, and by six o'clock we were already there. We were waiting for the bus to cross the border. We waited until nine o'clock, but the bus didn't arrive. Instead, more and more people came. A queue formed, women with children first, then everyone else. When we saw this kilometer-long line, we decided to walk. We had thirteen kilometers to go, with the suitcases . . . Thank God, at the ninth kilometer, a minibus picked us up and we walked the rest of the way. By the time we got to the border around noon, I was exhausted, my legs were killing me and my hands were blistered. We queued up to cross the border. We got through the Ukrainian border post very quickly, but we had to queue for a few hours at the Polish border post, and in winter, those few hours felt like a whole day. Thanks to the staff who served us hot meals, the hot soup came just in time! Shortly afterward, we crossed the Polish border. The question now was: how to continue? We were put on a bus and set off in an unknown direction. We then learned that we were being taken to a transit point, from where people would then be dispersed. A volunteer called out the direction the buses were going, and everyone who wanted to go raised their hand. Then I heard Berlin and immediately raised my hand! Berlin is indeed the capital of Germany, and it would already be closer to our final destination, Ahaus. I was delighted. However, our traveling companion didn't want to come with us, as she had arranged to meet her acquaintances in Poland and spend the night with them. And so our paths diverged. As we got off the bus, I saw a photographer taking pictures of everyone getting off. Immediately, terrible images from World War II films came to mind, of prisoners being taken on freight trains to concentration camps, to certain death. I tried to repress these terrible images and smiled at the camera. "Maybe one day this photo will feature in a history textbook," I said to myself.

We were standing next to the bus, looking for a sign that said "Berlin." Eventually, I saw a tall, athletic man with a promising "Berlin" sign. He looked at us and asked in Russian: "Do you want to go to Berlin? Are you expected there?" I replied that we wanted to go to North Rhine-Westphalia, that we were expected there, and that Berlin was the fastest way to get there. After some thought, he agreed to help us. On the way to the car, we made our introductions. Another young man, his son, was waiting for us by the car. They put our suitcases in the trunk and off we went! On the way, we learned that they had come from Berlin to Przemyśl to look for their Kyiv acquaintances who, like us, had had to flee the war. However, something had gone wrong and they didn't come. And so as not to leave empty-handed, they decided to take other people with them, and we were the lucky ones that day. We were lucky to meet such nice people. We'd been on the road a long time, but we'd already calmed down inside. From time to time, the phrase "we're alive" came to mind.

We arrived in Berlin in the evening and were greeted by a very hospitable young family, who gave us a separate room, made the beds, and provided us with everything we needed. Dinner was cooking. It was warm and comfortable. I went for a shower. It was so nice to be under hot water... The meal was already ready, but we didn't have much of an appetite after our arduous journey. My mother stayed in the room, and I just had a cup of hot tea and a chat with the people who had helped us through this difficult time. I would like to thank them, especially for that! It was a lovely evening with nice people! We chatted some more, then I fell into a warm, cozy bed, exhausted. We slept soundly and were well-rested the next morning. All the previous day's guests had already left, leaving only our hostess, her daughter, and the au pair. We were treated to a delicious meal, the likes of which I would never had before. It was traditional French cuisine. It was delicious... Afterward, we walked around Berlin together for a while, then our hostess personally drove us to the station and put us on the train to Hamm, where we changed trains for Münster. In the evening, when we arrived in Münster, my friend was already waiting for us! He ran up to us on the platform and gave me a big hug, with a smile on his face! It was so beautiful. At home, everything was ready for us: we each had our own room with new sheets. A cooked dinner was on the table. It was very pleasant and convivial.

When I woke up the next morning, I lay in bed for a long time thinking about everything we'd been through in that short time. I still couldn't believe that in our time, people were again experiencing missile explosions and that I had to wake up thinking: "IN UKRAINE, IT IS WAR!!!"

[Author's note: Yana]

By Adelina Mokliak

Date of birth: June 18, 1996
From: Kharkiv
Profession: Musician
First encounter with war: January 2014 at the Euromaidan in Kyiv
In Kyiv at the start of the invasion; escaped to Berlin

November 3, 2022

About a month before the invasion, my female friends and I created the Emergency Kit chat, but none of us took the threat of war seriously. On the chat, we exchanged jokes, we planned to buy flowers together, and we chatted about everything except the war. We had no particular plan. We just wanted to live. We had many common projects, creative and every day, for the near future. On the eve of the war, we agreed on this chat to go and see a film in the evening at my friend's house. I remember it like it was yesterday. It was a thriller in two parts, but I got tired almost immediately, just after the first part. It was about ten o'clock in the evening. The night before the war, I went home earlier than usual. I went to bed and fell sound asleep.

In the morning, I was awakened by vibrations. My mother called four times on my mobile, and I didn't answer any of the four calls. I stayed in bed for a while, then decided to open Telegram. My friend Olia, who had been away studying in Paris for a while, wrote to me, very curtly, something like this: "The war has started, you know?" It was about half past five. I called my mother back. She told me that Boryspil airport had been bombed half an hour before and that she'd heard explosions from our apartment in Kharkiv, and she said she wouldn't leave Kharkiv. She told me to pack immediately. Then I called my chat friends seven times. They were a couple at the time. I finally woke them up and started packing one suitcase, then a second, slowly and carefully. I wasn't scared yet, but I realized that I might never come back to this apartment.

About an hour later, I went out and looked for my car. I don't know why, but I'd completely forgotten where I'd parked it the day before. I got behind the wheel, the tank was full and I'd already changed the oil a few weeks earlier. I was very happy and drove to the front of the house so I wouldn't have to drag my suitcases too far. In addition to the suitcases, I took along a pool cue, a gift from my mother, who had taught me to play when I was just old enough to reach the table.

On the way to the girls' home, I picked up one of them, Bohdana, at an ATM in central Kyiv. We had a coffee and something to eat. The girls didn't want to leave, so I said I'd leave for Berlin tomorrow morning anyway. We got into the car and went to our shared studio. One of the girls, Alina, was making sculptures there, I was making music in the next room and our friend Antigona was projecting video art in the third room. In the studio, we were always hooked on our cell phones. Someone suggested we go to the Bunker, a well-known club on Kyrylivska Street. I joked: "Let's go to the Berghain right away." Nikita Kadan, a well-known Ukrainian artist, joined us, we bought some booze and started drinking heavily. Once we were drunk, I started slowly packing up the record players and synthesizers. The girls offered to fetch a minibus to take away the sculptures and records and evacuate as many people as possible. Already very drunk, we headed for the minibus, which was painted in every color. No one but me could drive, so I got behind the wheel, only to realize that I couldn't start it because the bus had a manual gearbox. The owner explained to me on the phone what I had to do, and then we started up and drove home without stopping. When we got home, I realized we'd had a flat tire, and when I looked under the hood, I saw oil as black as pitch. So we could forget about taking the minibus. We looked at the air-raid shelter, which was full of frightened people, and realized that our only option was to leave the next morning.

On the morning of February 25, everything was foggy. The girls were crying and packing. The GPS told us to leave the symbolic city via the Victory Avenue, but there was a huge traffic jam with heavy vehicles. We didn't know who these tanks belonged to, coming out of the forest on the outskirts of Kyiv.

Three girls in a Subaru Impreza, Bohdana, Alina, and I, left the country without a plan. Fortunately, Bohdana's stepfather, a cartographer, had prepared the route with the fewest traffic jams. In Bila Zerkva, thirty kilometers from Kyiv, one of my colleagues pointed out a gas station where there was still petrol, whereas the other stations had already run out. We bought several five-liter cans of windshield washer fluid. Bohdana used them to fill the windscreen washers of the other cars in line. We took along thirty liters of gasoline in these plastic cans, then another ten liters in two-liter Coca-Cola bottles. I called my mother and asked if we could smoke in the car, and she said she had done so in the '90s. I decided we wouldn't smoke.

Then came the bombing of the town of Vinnytiya, where Antigona, our studio's third user, happened to be staying. There was no more room in the car, but we decided to go and get her anyway and put her on the Technics 1210 MKII turntable. We called the place "Quasimodo" in reference to Notre-Dame de Paris because the person there had to curl up like a hunchback.

Fifty kilometers before Vinnytsia, a huge traffic jam was ahead of us and, given our general tiredness and lack of petrol, we decided not to get into the traffic jam, but to drive to the next village and seek shelter there until the next morning. It was a tiny village with just one street. At the end of the street, I saw a door open and a light in the window. I got out of the car and knocked on the window. A man in his forties, armed with a rifle, opened the door. I explained our situation and asked to stay the night. He listened to me and demanded to see my passport. He called his mother, and then our car, accompanied by a group of ten armed men, representatives of the territorial defense, slowly made its way to another house where an elderly woman prepared two beds for us in two spare rooms. In the morning, we ate soup, watched President Zelensky's speech on TV with the old woman, and offered her money for spending the night, but she refused, so we thanked her and left.

When we got back on the Vinnytsia-Ternopil freeway, the traffic jams had lengthened even further and we were moving even more slowly. Suddenly, I noticed some 4x4s and a few cars heading into the forest on an old single-lane paved road. As our car was four-wheel-drive, we went that way too. It was the worst seventy kilometers of my life. Every ten seconds the car floor hit the cobblestones. Brush scratched the doors on both sides. I drove at a snail's pace, with no cell phone reception. For almost three hours we moved slowly along the line of cars, the girls sometimes in tears. Then it was over, and we arrived in Ternopil, a town further west in the Ukraine. During an air alert, Alina had the "brilliant" idea of going immediately to the military police station to join the Ukrainian armed forces. There, Alina lined up with her diploma from the Academy of Design and Art. Bohdana and I were a bit apart, and I started laughing loudly and hysterically. Bohdana tried to calm me down. The police station was full of strong men who were probably surprised by my reaction. An hour later, Alina was expelled, we got into the car and left for L'viv.

We stayed in L'viv for a week. It was quite quiet, hardly anyone paid any attention to the air raid alarm. Once, we called the police because we thought a saboteur was living in our house. He was a taciturn man who never greeted us.

At the end of the week, Alina's mother called us and asked us to make some posters for the billboards along the highway that runs from Kharkiv to Belgorod (Russia) and that heavy vehicles used to use to get to Kharkiv. We started brainstorming. "Surrender is more honorable than death," "Does your mother know where you are?" The slogans came quickly and spontaneously to mind. Then, for the first time in several days, I turned on my laptop to watch Russian propaganda, perhaps it would be wiser to imagine something in their language for these soldiers. After all, our main objective was to stop them. How naive, how pacifist. I realize that now.

As I worked in the IT field, I quickly noticed, after connecting to the Internet, that my processor was slowing down and my RAM was overloaded with unknown processes. We checked the connection history on Telegram and Facebook and found that three of our four phones had been connected from places we didn't know. I then told the girls that we would leave for Poland first thing in the morning because if the network was hacked, I would no longer be able to work, earn a living, and help my mother. This was unimaginable for me, especially under wartime conditions.

Bohdana absolutely wouldn't leave, so Alina and I agreed that if we had no other choice, we'd tie her up. Alina even prepared some ropes. We started gathering our things in the car from the rented apartment in L'viv. Alina decided to leave her biggest suitcase behind so she could take more people to the border. It later turned out that she had also left Bohdana's suitcase with her childhood photo album in the hallway. In the car, we were listening to Okean Elsy, Ukraine's most dramatic pop-rock band, and heading for the Krakovets border crossing when, thirty kilometers from the border, Alina suddenly wanted to jump out of the car window at a checkpoint. We stopped and tried to calm her down. She took an irritant spray out of her bag and started spraying it in our eyes. The policemen at the checkpoint saw this, came over, and tied Alina to a post and called an ambulance. Antigona stood beside the car and made the sign of the cross. Alina, tied up, was placed in the ambulance, we turned around and also went to the hospital. The injection of a sedative and three hours of conversation weren't enough to bring her to her senses. she wanted to return to L'viv, but Alina's father sent someone for her and she was admitted to a psychiatric hospital where she stayed for the next two weeks. We spat and cried because of the spray; the tears wouldn't stop flowing. We crossed the border, arrived in Krakow, and checked into a hotel. I decided to stay in the same room as Bohdana, and we've been living together ever since. I love her, first and foremost as a friend, but sometimes also in the evenings. That's why this story isn't so dramatic for me, even if my left eye still sees a little less well than my right.

We've been living in Berlin for eight months now. At first, I liked everything about it and was convinced that the choice of a life without war was the right one. The fact is, it's impossible to choose a life without war when in your country a fierce struggle for freedom is waged every day, a defensive war that claims hundreds of victims every day. More and more news reached me about the deaths of people I knew personally. My mother remained in Kharkiv, renovating the cellar that she and her neighbors had been using as an air-raid shelter all this time. Our house is right in the center, near the Kharkiv local administration building, and our house is the only one in the whole neighborhood that still has windows. One day, I stopped believing my mother and asked her to send me video evidence. Because every morning I wake up and read the news, and it's usually bad. I feel like there's no more good news in this world.

I must remind you that I'm only 26. For the last three months, I've been in a very bad way, waking up every morning at half past five because I can't sleep, and I'm already looking forward to my appointment at the Charité hospital at the end of November. Permanent anxiety is taking up more and more space in my life, and more and more of my time. The main reason is, of course, everything

that's going on at the moment, and especially the fact that there's nothing I can do about it. I'm still paying taxes in Ukraine. My salary is losing more and more of its value due to inflation, but although I'm getting lots of offers for other jobs, I can't change. I can't help but give my country what I have. I can't help but support those who defend our country. I can't help reading the terrible news every day. I can't help worrying more and more about the lack of electricity in Ukraine, about the critical infrastructure being bombed. I haven't seen the bombs with my own eyes, the horrific abuse of civilians, the missiles, and the ruins. I feel them all the same. It's like a phantom pain that will probably stay with me forever. Would I like to stay in Germany for the rest of my life? No, of course not. More than anything else in the world, I want to return to Ukraine, to my peaceful Kyiv, to visit my mother in Kharkiv. I want to walk the streets I did when I was a little girl. That's no longer possible because all those streets are destroyed, there's nothing left but ruins, and even my old school is in ruins. Germany is a beautiful country, of course, but when you're forced to move, you never feel at home anywhere. And everything you've achieved for yourself seems insignificant when Russia is firing missiles at your town at the same time. Yesterday, there were fifty missiles. "Massive missile attack" has been the most used expression all these months. In second place is "nuclear war."

Russia says it's fighting Nazism. This is simply absurd. I have Jewish roots and I know what Nazism is, if only because my family was forced to change its surname during the Second World War. I believe that Nazism itself has made mankind violently reject it. On this point too, the Kremlin has invented nothing new. And that an aggressor could simply reinterpret terms to such an extent as to indoctrinate the population of an entire country and wage a bloody war, I can't believe. I can't believe that in 2022, we'll be living through such misfortune. Bombs, missiles, and artillery are hitting museums, libraries, and universities—institutions that cannot easily be rebuilt—children from the occupied territories are being forcibly relocated to Russia, and there are civilian casualties every day. Does this sound familiar? What indications are still needed to stop this bloody genocide?

I don't understand how all this could happen and why. Above all, I don't understand what mankind has done to make it all happen. For eight months, Europe has been in the grip of a bloody war, and no one can stop it. This war has taken from me so many things I built with my own hands day after day, everything I loved so much, and now this war is starting to take from me day after day those I love. I am convinced that one day we will be victorious and that racism will be punished, and I hope that this will be the last manifestation of ethnic nationalism in the world. We, that is Ukrainians, Jews, all peoples and nations. A coalition of victors can put an end to it once and for all.

By Olga Afanasyeva

Date of birth: March 3, 1986
From: Sumy
Profession: Director of the ELEKS branch in Kyiv
In Southern Italy at the start of the invasion

August 8, 2022

At the end of January 2022, I was lying on a sofa in southern Italy, wondering how I could have broken my foot almost at ground level. It was the first fracture of my life, and I'm not a fan of extreme sports. I felt like Joey from Friends who, on his thirtieth birthday, looks up at the ceiling and says: "My God, why? We had an agreement. We agreed that I wouldn't break anything, that I'd do yoga, and that I wouldn't ski!"

In February, I wanted to go to Kyiv and Sumy to visit my family, my workplace, and my home. The fracture put an end to my travel plans and I barely managed to get to the next room by hopping on one leg.

The story of how the war caught me where I could be most useful began on December 30. After celebrating Catholic Christmas with my parents in northeastern Ukraine, my husband and I were on our way to southern Italy. We wanted to celebrate New Year's Eve in his country. En route, we talked about the war which, according to my husband's theory, would start very soon. I disagreed. After all, we Ukrainians had been living with war in Ukraine for eight years, and we weren't so easily impressed. It was exhausting to think and talk about it, and it didn't really seem necessary, even though we were preparing for this scenario at work.

The other topic of conversation during the three-thousand-kilometer trip was dogs. We had talked at length about the joy of owning a pug. Of course, I wanted one, but in my head, discussions about it were as remote as the possibility of a full-scale attack on my homeland by our neighboring country.

To cut down on travel time (or so I thought), my husband suggested we look up refugees on the Internet and give them a call. We crossed most of Italy from top to bottom, a unique opportunity to stop in almost every town. After about two dozen calls, we were told somewhere near Florence that there were two-month-old puppies and that we could drop by. A few hours before arriving home, we found our dog and the three of us set off to celebrate New Year's Eve.

The course of our stay in Italy therefore had to be adapted. The new plan now included obtaining documents and vaccinations for the dog, without which we couldn't enter Ukraine. In other words, we had planned to stay in Italy until the end of January. But then the return to Kyiv was also postponed because of my broken foot...

And so, in February 2022, there I was, reflecting on all these atypical circumstances in my life. I couldn't understand how or why this had happened to me. My last doctor's appointment was scheduled for the evening of February 24...

A few days before the war, there was already fear in the air. The foreboding of something terrible was almost physically perceptible. On the evening of February 23, we learned that one of the founders of the company we worked for had died suddenly at work. It was a total shock for all of us. Our company was founded by a family of engineers and is as old as independent Ukraine—we celebrated thirty years of existence last autumn.

We had agreed to an online brainstorming meeting for the following day at nine o'clock. The meeting didn't take place as planned.

February 24: that was the start of an interminable day that lasted for months. And is probably still going on. As in peacetime, my father left for work as usual, and I couldn't wait for him to come home to reassure me a little. My hometown lies directly on the border with the aggressor state. The region was considered "uninteresting."

When I think back on everything that's happened, it's pretty hard to recount it in a linear way. What's more, my brain is configured in such a way that it always finds inspiring and positive moments in past events that I want to keep in my memory, while I want to repress catastrophic events. But as Ernest Hemingway wrote: "There's nothing worse than war." Unfortunately, we've had the opportunity to experience just that.

The morning the war started, I understood why (perhaps) my departure for Ukraine had been delayed by the dog and the broken foot. Higher forces must have discovered that the keyboard and the Internet were my most powerful weapons.

Early on the morning of February 24, we began helping friends and colleagues in the eastern and central regions, as well as in Kyiv, to find transport and coordinate travel itineraries. In the first few weeks, several hundred of our colleagues and their families traveled to the western part of Ukraine and beyond.

For the first three months, I was always awake at around four or five in the morning to find out about the situation in my hometown of Sumy. I'd wake up my mother and, once I'd heard that everything was fine, I'd continue sleeping until eight o'clock, when I'd go back to work.

We tried to keep in touch with our family. We tried to find a balance between reassuring our loved ones (I'm not sure we succeeded) and our own feelings about the constant flow of news. I think tears were coming every hour, I'd almost got used to it.

I have to say that my family refused to leave despite many attempts at persuasion. Work, responsibility, hometown. It's very difficult to accept that your parents are adults and have the right to make their own decisions.

Understanding

In the morning, our friends from Kyiv left to join us in southern Italy. It was the beginning of total war, and panic was everywhere. Our friends didn't have any car insurance to cross the border, so I helped them buy some online. I found a website, applied for insurance, and was waiting for the e-mail from the police.

Time passes. As I still had no reply to my e-mail, I went back to the site and shouted at the online support box. After a while, I received a reply from a member of staff: "Sorry for the delay, there was an alarm and we were in the air-raid shelter . . . I'm sending this to the police immediately. I'm sending this to the police immediately."

Nowadays, you don't get surprised by things like that. But that was the first day, and I understood right away what was going on.

For the first few weeks, my hometown and the surrounding area were blocked by the occupiers. Entry, exit, and deliveries were impossible. The first "green corridors" were targeted. There were also deaths. It was around this time that my cousin and I began active volunteering. I was outside Ukraine, he was in the country. Finding diapers, non-perishable food, first-aid kits, etc., was another important part of our new reality.

We couldn't just pick things up and send them, or send a car to Sumy. Experience in project management, logistics, and stress management was definitely needed for all of us, and we acquired it. And that's when I really felt our unity. It was like being in a movie: you ask for help and colleagues or strangers look for ways to help without asking too many questions. And vice versa.

For us, what is at stake in this war is the great humanity of the Ukrainian people, unity, and faith. Such ordinary words. And such strong feelings.

About Work

The work was a great help. It gave meaning to endless sleepless days and scrolling messages in Telegram groups.

At work, we organized daily meetings with colleagues from Kyiv and the eastern regions, so that all those who needed support—both physical and moral—knew that this common space existed. Over time, everyone got more or less used to the situation (people get used to everything over time) and weekends were free.

Back then, this was the most difficult phase—too much free time. Watching the news and asking parents, "How are you?" was the only way to fill the void.

But was this the right thing to do? That's why, in a way, Monday was always a relief. We're busy with work. And so we have less time for other thoughts and worries. Who'd have thought it—checkmate for stereotypes.

Birthday

On March 3, the second week of the war began. It was my birthday. A very strange time. Wishes are gifts to support the hometown. The best gift is freedom from worry. The greatest dream is that the war will be over and loved ones safe.

The day was more or less calm. (Or should I add that with the start of the war, the number of heartbeats per minute had adapted to the alarms in the hometown? The Apple Watch could already use an update to take this into account.) Going out to party at night was a strange idea, but my husband and family had almost convinced me to go out for the first time in two months . . .

That same evening, the electricity substation in my hometown was hit by artillery fire. All communications, electricity, water, and heating were cut off (in March, it's still very cold in northern Ukraine). Okay, we stayed home; all the alarms were going off. Alarms in every sense of the word.

Butsha

Over time, we all got more or less used to what was going on. It became business as usual. I remember when I gave myself moral permission to go for a walk in the open air and mute some Telegram groups. I went into the living room where the TV was on. The news on Butsha. That day, the Kyiv-region town had been liberated after a month of occupation, and journalists were publishing shocking photos and videos of the torture that had taken place there. Numerous murders and shattered lives, the enemy's inhuman war crimes. As the saying goes, "We thought we'd reached the ground, but it hit from below."

The rabbit and the spider

If I'm writing about women in war, I should also mention the rescue of female animals from the loneliness of war.

In peacetime, Lola the rabbit and Matilda the spider lived in our Kyiv office. When the war broke out, the office was closed and the only person to look after them in the early days was the janitor. When all our colleagues were more or less safe, we launched an action to save the animals. The rabbit was brought by friends to our office in Western Ukraine, the terrarium with the spider Matilda was left with the janitor at his request, as they had already become good friends.

Coincidences that are not accidental

A lot happened for the first time. An online course for students from all over Ukraine was interrupted by an air alert. Is it appropriate to talk about venture capital investment when there's war all around?

The happiest moment of the war was when we managed to meet my parents after five months of conflict. There are no words to describe the happiness felt at that reunion. These are the happiest moments in life, and you want to keep them to yourself.

In fact, I still managed to make it to the doctor's appointment on the evening of the 24th. I always thought it would be one of the happiest days of my life, that I'd be able to walk with both legs again! I had no idea that this war would still be going on as I write this in the late summer of 2022.

When I was able to read books after the outbreak of large-scale war, I turned to the famous classics of the war novel. I found it interesting to reread them then and compare my feelings with what people were writing at the time of the world wars. Is there romance in war? It's not well known. And as I write these lines, I want to believe that the end of the war and victory are near. For as the missiles fly, we should all remember the words of Jeannette Pickering Rankin, the American women's rights activist who was the first woman in the US Congress to cast the lone vote against the country's entry into both world wars: "You can no more win a war than you can win an earthquake."

[Author's note: Olga relocated to Poland on her own in 2022, while her family remains residing in Sumy.]

By Anastasiya Gruba

Date of birth: August 11, 1996
From: Kyiv
Profession: Scriptwriter
In Kyiv at the start of the invasion; fled to Western Ukraine and returned to Kyiv in April, 2022

August 11, 2022

"To the dead, to the living, and to those not yet born..."

Today, I'm twenty-six years old. Ukraine will soon be thirty-one years old, and the war will soon be six months old. So far, I've been lucky enough to survive. Many Ukrainians haven't... I hate myself for that. The collective pain is so strong that it takes my breath away and can be felt in my feet. I'm torn between an unreal desire for peace and a real, terrible war.

I realize that I'm not a heroine. To be honest, I expected more from myself. I didn't become a rescue worker, I didn't actively volunteer, and I didn't even stay in my hometown when the full-scale invasion began. I was scared, confused, and not myself. I know this is normal, but I still feel ashamed.

The war surprised me at home, in bed. First an explosion, then a call from my mother. At first, I wasn't afraid. For the first time since my little accident, I got behind the wheel and drove halfway across town to pick up a friend. Kyiv seemed nervous but serene. People were trying not to panic, but to be considerate and polite to each other. They listened carefully to the noises and looked intently at the sky. We had the feeling that this war wouldn't last long, that everything would soon be settled, and that all we had to do was wait a day or two. The world could not allow such a bloody war to break out again in Europe...

Yet the world let it happen. War has broken out. And what do I feel? I don't feel anything anymore. All Ukrainians have experienced so much pain and hatred during these six months that it's enough to last a lifetime. I think that after the terrible bombardments of the cities, after the events in Butsha, Irpin, and Borodianka, after the reports from Mariupol and the online broadcasts from the Azov steelworks, my body decided to freeze the feelings so as not to be disturbed.

Yet, alongside the hatred and pain, there was and still is another feeling—love, a great, pure, deep love. Love for all Ukrainians who united against the enemy, who supported each other, who believed in victory, even when the whole world was convinced that the terrible Great Russia would take over Ukraine in... when? In a week? Ukrainians are a nation of free men. We are very attached to freedom, and that's why we still exist. The countries that tried to conquer us have disappeared from the world map, but we're here, and we'll stay here. I'm sure it's this collective love that will lead us to victory. It's our source of energy that cannot be destroyed. Because the more we are beaten, the stronger our cohesion.

I spent the first weeks of the war in a dacha near Kyiv with my family, my boyfriend, and my female friend. Those were the most terrible days of my life, even if I didn't realize it at the time. We were very close to the combat zone.

We could hear enemy tanks in the streets. We saw fighter planes flying over the roof. We lived with the sound of explosions, which were omnipresent. We felt a rocket whistle so loud and so close that the whole house shook. We saw the red sky above the exploded oil depot in Vasyl'kiv. We learned how to make Molotov cocktails from Facebook posts because we had no other weapons. We extinguished a field after our artillery destroyed Russian tanks there. Neighbors would come and spend the night in our cellar when the surrounding sounds of fighting were louder and scarier than usual. We would go to the nearest village to buy milk and bread, and we were really getting ready to starve. We fell asleep with the cell phone in hand and woke up to the news. We didn't get changed before going to bed, because we knew we had to be ready at any moment to reach the shelter quickly. So we slept on and off, for two or three hours at a time. We were six adults, two children, two cats, and a dog.

Explosions multiplied in the surrounding area. We knew the occupants were only a few kilometers from our village. We could hear them. My younger brother (aged nine) was constantly shaking with fear. We couldn't hold out any longer and decided to take the risk. We decided to leave before it was too late. We headed west in two cars filled with people, animals, and goods. We knew that there were hardly any safe roads left, but we were lucky.

It sounds like a thriller or a horror film. Doesn't it? But compared to what other Ukrainians have gone through or are still going through, it's just a children's story. Occupation, filtration camp, captivity. Behind these words lie atrocities so inhuman they're impossible to describe. Generally speaking, I have the feeling that every horror described in words is devalued, mitigated, no longer so horrible, and somehow seems more acceptable. For the moment, this war is simply incomprehensible, both to those who live it and to those who watch it from afar. Humanity will only be able to grasp all this in time.

Up until February 24, I had been working in the film industry, dreaming of writing new stories and even launching my own career as a director. The large-scale invasion wiped out all my plans and dreams. It was as if an A4 sheet filled with color had been completely erased and left blank. Throughout the spring, I wasn't myself. My feelings were changing so fast that I didn't have time to catch my breath. I was constantly tense. I did everything I could not to think about the news. I eagerly seized every opportunity to feel better, but I just couldn't do it. I pretended to control myself and my emotions, but in reality, I was like a frightened, stalked animal that, although it had already taken cover, simply couldn't calm down. It took me a while to come back to reality. It wasn't until summer that I could feel again that I had my roots, that I could be stable and not be at the mercy of emotional fluctuations, that I could face uncertainties

and find at least a little harmony within myself. In the end, it helped me to pick myself up and see what I wanted to do next and how I should go about it. For myself, my family, and my Ukraine. I'm on the road back to cinema, however long and thorny that road may be. I realized that it was my duty to tell as many stories as possible about the experiences of Ukrainians. And even though I may not be able to assess everything properly now, I want to keep a record of these moments so important to the Ukrainian nation and pass them on to the next generation.

I will not allow this war to be forgotten. On my birthday, I have only one wish, which everyone can guess. Glory to Ukraine!

[Author's note: In 2024, she released her debut short film, entitled Driving Lessons, which tells the story of one day in the life of a father and daughter in wartime Kyiv.]

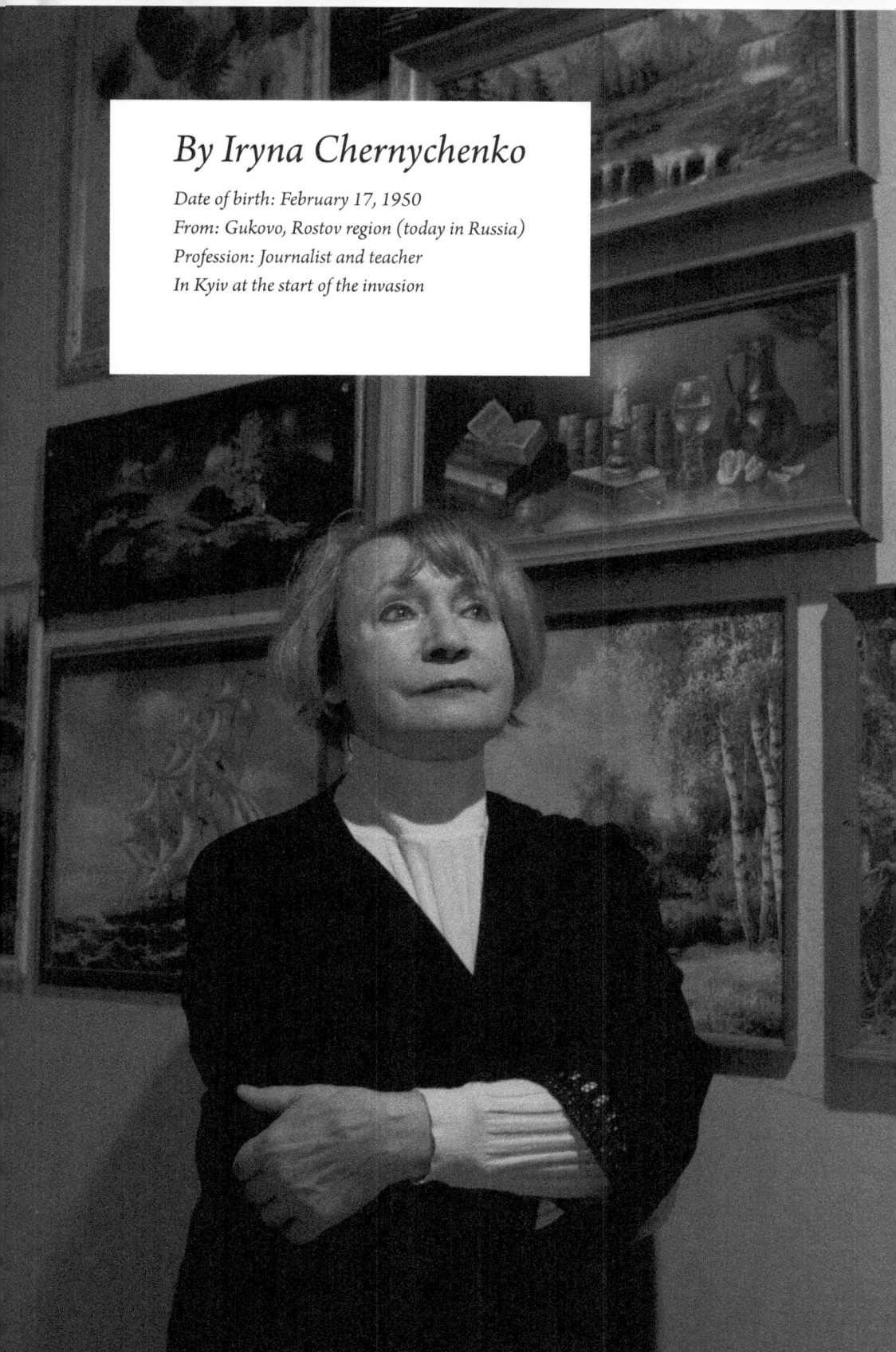

By Iryna Chernychenko

Date of birth: February 17, 1950
From: Gukovo, Rostov region (today in Russia)
Profession: Journalist and teacher
In Kyiv at the start of the invasion

September 18, 2022

For the past six months, the beautiful city of Kyiv, one of the most beautiful cities in the world, has been resounding with the terrible wail of sirens. It is war... But as beautiful as the capital is, I would rather go back to Donets'k, the peaceful Ukrainian Donets'k.

My parents' ancestors came from Ukraine: my mother's parents from the Poltava region, my father's from the Chernihiv region. It seems they had their reasons for taking refuge in the nineteenth century in the Don region, which was freer than the other regions of the Russian Empire.

I chose journalism when I was at school. I used to write articles for the local newspaper, and it was with these (my "portfolio") that I enrolled in the Faculty of Journalism at Moscow's Lomonosov State University. It was there that I met my husband, also an ethnic Ukrainian, and aser our studies, we moved together to Donets'k.

At the time, the city was predominantly Russian-speaking, and when I worked for state television, youth programs were broadcast in Russian. When I started working in radio in 1985, also at State Radio, Donetsk's Ukrainian cultural community began to grow in importance. More and more was being written in Ukrainian, and at meetings in museums and libraries, people began to talk about Ukrainian national roots, which go back a long way in the Donets'k region.

I understood that I had to learn the language properly and not just read books, as I had done when I arrived in Ukraine.

I didn't lose sight of the fact that I would soon be forty. Every day, I spent half an hour learning Ukrainian—with textbooks, dictionaries, and reading fiction aloud. I talked to friends and colleagues and asked them to correct me. At the time, a young professor at Donets'k University, Anatolii Sahnitko (now a professor and member of the Ukrainian National Academy of Sciences), had just been appointed director of the radio station's literary department, and he proposed a series of programs on the Ukrainian language and culture. For ten years, the program was broadcast once a month, with Anatolii Panassowytsch writing the script and hosting. At first, episodes consisted solely of his own texts and interviews with studio guests. Over time, radio programs became more lively and polyphonic overall. A five-minute program now also had to contain material recorded "on location." This "on location" was increasingly taking place in Donetsk's Ukrainian cultural life, at theatrical performances and literary events, in museums and libraries.

It took me six months to learn to speak Ukrainian, and then I started writing, reporting, and interviewing. That's why I know that it's possible to learn a language from A to Z, even as an adult, if you want to, and that knowledge always opens up interesting perspectives.

Since 1993, I've been teaching with growing passion. First I was invited to teach a radio journalism course at a private school, then I started training journalists at Donets'k National University, where I taught for almost twenty years. In June 2014, my students were still defending their degrees in Donets'k, but very soon the university was on the run (as were many of us). After we rallied together and mobilized our forces, the university was back in business by February, in Vinnytsia. Students followed, and professors also settled in Vinnytsia or commuted from other towns.

To support the university and meet the students, I made the trip from Kyiv twice a month for three or four days—which enabled me to give my classes.

Students often ask me: what do you prefer, journalism or teaching? I always answer that I like catamarans, because they guarantee stability, which is very important. I'm very grateful to my colleagues at the Department of Film Directing and Dramaturgy at the Kyiv National University of Theater, Film, and Television for inviting me to work there in 2019 when I couldn't travel to Vinnytsia as often due to health problems.

It was a new challenge because the areas of study are different: documentary, animation and fiction filmmaking, and dramaturgy. New courses, new teaching methods. Now, the war has scattered students all over Ukraine, and all over the world, and it's much harder to stay focused and attentive online than in a quiet or even more emotional conversation in a seminar room.

Then the war came to the lives of my students, some of whom can already be considered my friends. I remember my former student Azad telling me, about four years ago, that he had accompanied an American TV crew to the site where the remains of the Malaysia Airlines MH17 plane had been scattered. I was a little scared at the time, but I didn't need to be, because it was already done, it was over. Azad Safarov and I met again in Kyiv, halfway through his journey. He was on his way from Bonn, where he was working at the time, to the grey zone of Mariupol (a lawless place, controlled neither by Russian nor Ukrainian forces). At the time, he was there with Danish director Simon Wilmont, shooting *The Distant Barking of Dogs*. The film's main characters are a grandmother and her ten-year-old grandson, Oleh, who live in the village of Hnutowe. Five years in a village almost entirely destroyed, and gunshots are heard throughout the film.

For me, gunshots and barking dogs are particular metaphors. I asked how the director dealt with the circumstances in which filming took place. Azad's reply: "Simon says I've spent the night in a trench before, and this time he wants to do the same."

Two years later, Simon Wilmont and Azad Safarov shot another film, *A House Made of Splinters*. They had to travel again to eastern Ukraine, this time to a home for children in difficulty. They spoke with the children who spent nine months there before returning to their parents or being placed in a boarding school or foster family. While we were filming in the Luhansk region, the war was just around the corner, and now the occupying troops are there.

When I met Azad, some of his impressions became mine, and my concern for him grew because I knew he was not telling me everything . . . And because he always wants to be there for others, to help and do something, he's already been hurt during the Maidan events.

In August, Anton Lyagucha, another former student, colleague, and friend, returned to Kyiv from Washington. He had worked at George Mason University for a year, had received offers to extend his work in the United States, and still had a valid visa, but "at times like this, I should be here, with my country, my family, and my friends. I've helped the Ukrainian armed forces from there, but here I can do more."

We're constantly making decisions, but the events of 2014 forced me and those around me in Donets'k to opt for Ukraine once and for all. Of course, my friends had no doubts about who we were and who we were for, but leaving everything behind—our home, our favorite books, our memories—hanging in the void with no job or fixed accommodation, having to fend for ourselves in an environment that wasn't always friendly at the time, this decision took a lot of strength.

As late as April, we were on our way to pro-Ukrainian demonstrations, and then not only did fighting break out, but so did deaths. In the spring, friends and colleagues began to leave Donets'k. And when we were evicted from the Donets'k State TV a Radio building, I was stunned. The "little green men" had threatened us with weapons. It was perfectly clear that they were soldiers, not insurgents or snipers. The fact that I still had hope prevented me from leaving the city immediately. Our men were bound to arrive at any moment; they couldn't abandon us. In October 2014, I was already in Kyiv.

Some people (of different nationalities) weren't sure they were Ukrainian politically. They were all over Ukraine, not just in the east of the country as some people think. The explosions of February 24, 2022, brought everyone to a final decision. The majority united, managed to resist the enemy in a variety of ways, and began to get busy both at the front and in the rear. On the morning of that memorable February 24, I woke up to the sound of explosions. I not only heard them, I also saw them, because from the windows of my house in the north of Kyiv, I could see Pushcha Vodyzia, and next door, Butsha . . .

I learned that two of my friends and their families were already in a shelter in Butsha. They spent several weeks there and we didn't hear from them for a long time. Tension was high. Finally, Olena and her family made it to Kyiv, followed by Volodymyr and his son.

In comparison, we had only minor problems. If there was no bread, we would buy rusks, if the corner store was closed, we would go a little further afield, the shelves only empty or half-empty for a few days. Friends would share bread, apples, jam, whatever they had on hand—the gesture itself was the most important thing.

Yes, we have heard the explosions and seen on the Internet how, in the Kyiv region where we live, enemy vehicles rammed a car driven by an elderly man who miraculously survived. We have written about sabotage groups being put out of action nearby, and in the next street a multi-story building was destroyed by shellfire, but compared to the terrible losses suffered by others, it seems a sin to complain.

When all these horrors are over, when victory comes—and it will come anyway—I think the most terrible thing in many people's memories will remain the siren's wail, when you are overwhelmed by fear for your loved ones. No, it is not for me that I have been shaking for months when the siren wails! My grandson, a student, is with me. How can I protect him when everything is so unpredictable and there is hardly anywhere safe . . .

About five years ago, while working for a TV station in Kyiv (which has since been closed down), I mentioned one day while chatting with colleagues that I had a dacha near Donets'k, a plot of land with an incredible amount of flowers. "Where is your dacha?" I was asked. "Very close to Donets'k airport, not far from the village of Pisky," I replied. At the time, Donets'k airport was seen by many as a symbolic place: a symbol of resistance to the "cyborg" soldiers. Today, the name Pisky has taken on a special connotation, not least because of the fierce fighting around the village. Our soldiers are preventing the occupiers from taking it over completely—there are only nine inhabitants les—it is a strategic object, too close to Donets'k itself.

Hundreds of projectiles had already fallen on it, and someone tried to convince me that there could be no more life on our land. But I believe in the fantastic resilience of living plants. They can't disappear. The first to welcome me in spring was the big blue flowers of the periwinkle and, next to them, on the dogwood, a big ball of yellow flowers, like a reminder of the national flag.

Resistant like the Ukrainians. We will win and the plants will recover.

By Kristina Parioti

Date of birth: September 11, 2002
From: Mariupol
Profession: Philology student
In Mariupol at the start of the invasion; escaped with her mother and brother on April 14, 2022 to Ingolstadt, Germany

June 30, 2022

"The good life is wherever we happen not to be." We often hear something like this in our daily lives. But if we cross one word out, the phrase gets another meaning: "The good life is wherever we happen to be."

These words helped me and my family get out of the hell we ended up in, namely Mariupol. The war overtook us unexpectedly, as it did the whole country, but there are some cities that suffered the worst, where there is nowhere to live now. That is exactly what Mariupol has become.

It was a beautiful city by the sea, where peace and tranquility reigned and everyone lived measuredly, at their own pace. Everyone had their own goals and plans, dreams that all became secondary on February 24, when many questions about the future, and even the next day, suddenly came to the foreground. I would like to share my story so that people who have lost hope can hear it and continue to live, if not as before, then in a different way. Again.

In war, as in any stressful situation, it is important to be able to maintain a sober mind and not let anxiety, fear, and panic control you, as happened to many in Ukraine and led to a worsening of the situation. On the morning of February 24, instead of logging onto online classes at the university, my mind was occupied with thoughts about the war, about the future of our country, but not about myself and my city. No one expected the war to reach such catastrophic proportions and have such terrible consequences.

After what happened, namely Russia's invasion of Ukrainian territory, my family and I heard explosions and read the news 24/7, which only added to the alarm. My family is small: There is just my mother, younger brother, and me. My father has not lived in Ukraine for a long time. He lives in Russia, and though politics has never touched us, he knows which side is the truth. In the following days, my family and I stayed at home, even under heavy artillery fire, because in our house the basement was unsuitable for shelter. After a time, when the shelling intensified, we were forced to go to a nearby basement, next to my grandfather's (my mother's father's) home in a five-story building. Until that moment, those who were present in my daily life every day had been with me: my boyfriend and cat. We tried to keep calm, but it was impossible while reading the news every day. My family and I went to the basement and we barely saw my boyfriend, the cat was at home with full bowls of food, without the need for a person.

My relationship with this young man had had a long history. We had to go through a lot to finally achieve that calmness and tenderness in our relationship, but it came at an inopportune period. As my boyfriend had served before, when mobilization began in Ukraine, he was forced to apply for military registration and enlistment office for further instructions. On February 28, after going to the draft board, he was told that they would call back when needed, and they called him the same day. On that day we saw him for the last time.

At the beginning of March, my family and I stayed in the basement along with other families and acquaintances from the area, hoping every evening that this would be the last time. Everyone hoped that the government would resolve the conflict through diplomacy, and that everyone would be able to return home from the basements to their normal lives. But in early March, new shells hit Mariupol, as a result of which the city was left without water, gas, electricity, light, and communications.

For the next 20 days, we stayed and slept in basements, cooked on a fire under airstrikes, did not see the sunlight, and lived with the false hope that everything would end tomorrow and we only had to "wait a couple of days." Ukrainians learned to understand this phrase very well.

From time to time, my brother and I ran to our house to pick up the necessary things. We fed the cat and took important documents, food, and clothes, back amid the explosions. The weather conditions were not the best. Sleeping in the basement on wooden boards in a winter coat and our shoes at minus twelve degrees. I continually thanked God for life and for one more day in this cold, dusty, dark, gray, stuffy basement, which protected me and my family from the apocalypse above, from tanks that drove right between the courtyards of residential buildings, from airstrikes that left craters three meters deep. I thanked God for the opportunity to live, while many other people had already been deprived of that forever.

This continued until March 20. During this period, many people began to fuss and left, despite the risk, despite the fact that there were no green humanitarian corridors, and the Russian military was killing civilians with signs reading "children" on their cars. Little by little, day by day, the basement began to empty, there were fewer and fewer people, and then an inner miserable feeling of helplessness awoke in me. Even those who did not have a driving license left. The cars were broken and the gasoline was minimal, phones were charged from a car battery, and rainwater was saved. Everyone saved as much as they could. In the war, each person revealed their essence. Some could share their last piece of food, and some hid it and ate it themselves. And there were cases of looting. I wanted to get out of this hell, this chaos, this place where corpses were lying on the street among burnt houses and abandoned people. I asked God for the opportunity to get out of there. One day, he gave it to me. Early in the morning, a man came to our yard who was going to pick up his family from the other side of Mariupol. But the military wouldn't let him go there to save his family, so he had space for three people heading for Zaporizhzhia. I acted quickly. But my mother silently stood next to the car and did not collect her things, only watched as other people got in. They were able to leave and get to another city safely. That morning was the peak climax. I begged my family to pack their bags and leave the city on foot, as this was the only way to escape. There was no point staying there because we knew no one would come to the rescue. Without a car but with a driver's license, we ourselves would have gladly left, but there was no such possibility.

My mother did this because she had a choice between saving the children and leaving her father there, or staying with him. People didn't want to leave the city for several reasons that upset me: attachment to home; attachment to relatives; feeling as though they were not needed in other cities.

When my brother and I ran home amid the shooting for the last time, we moved the cat to our grandfather's apartment closer to the basement, took the most necessary things, and packed up to leave on foot. The night before our departure was exciting, what to expect was unknown. And then the morning of March 23 came. We collected all our things and said goodbye to our grandfather, I hugged the cat for the last time and we left with what we could carry. When we walked along the street, there was fighting on the next street, but there was no way back. Mom walked with tears in her eyes from the pain of leaving everything that was dear to her in exchange for saving her life. We reached the checkpoint that led into the unoccupied territory of Ukraine. That is, we managed to get from Mariupol to Berdyans'k in one day, taking into account the route on foot and evacuation buses.

Already that evening, I could charge my phone and get a signal. Immediately, the first person I called was my father, who for about a month had not known what was happening to us and whether we were alive. Dad now calls that day his second birthday, because we were able to get out of there and survive. Then there was the question of where to go, but the answer was clear in my head: Germany. Thanks to my education and knowledge of English and German, we decided to go there, into the unknown but to safety. We were on the road for about a week. Eventually, we saw the light of street lamps and better conditions, and little by little began to recover. When I finally arrived in Germany and reached my destination, I couldn't stop thinking about my boyfriend. In the basement, I tried not to think about him so as not to worry. He had told me that the best thing I could do for him was not to worry. So that was what I did, though it was extremely difficult, except perhaps for his sake. After a week of settling in Germany, suddenly God heard my prayers and my boyfriend wrote to me. It was the first message I had had from him since February 28.

My heart began to beat again as before at the appearance of those messages from him. When he sent me a photo of his injury, I realized that if it were not for that he would not have been able to write. That was the price he had to pay to be able to say that he was alive. When I learned that he was in a military hospital at Azovstal, I had nothing to say to him except how much I was proud of him and admired his courage and bravery, how much I loved him, and how much I missed him.

Our relationship had only grown stronger. Like never before, I wanted to hug him and never let go, but it was impossible. Being on a train, a bus, moving away from home with every step, I had moved away from him too. When he had the opportunity he wrote, but then for a long time he did not. The last time we talked with him was in April, and now it is already June. From the news we heard about the horrors that happened at Azovstal, and how people died there every day, but I continued to believe and pray. Once, a friend sent me a video with a note saying to turn it on at a certain second. Subconsciously, I understood that he would be there and that it would feel like the moment of our last meeting. I turned on the video and saw him. My heart bled from knowing that he was alive and, although injured, courageously continuing to hold on. Now, being safe, making every possible effort to help him get out of captivity and return home, I understand how much I loved him.

Occasionally more and more photos of our area appeared on the internet. It turned out that we had left just in time. There was nothing left of our building. It was completely burned down. When people ask me about the future, I am confused and don't know what to answer, because if I go back to Ukraine, it would not be to Mariupol. There is nothing there.

One story deserves special attention. As mentioned earlier, my father lives in Russia, and for about a month he did not hear any news about us or our condition, or whether we were alive at all. After we talked to him in Berdyans'k for the first time, we kept in touch throughout our journey to Germany. My parents have a beautiful love story and a complicated family life. They are divorced, but continue to communicate with each other respectfully. Learning that grandfather had stayed in Mariupol, our father promised to pick him up and made a decision to travel from St. Petersburg to Mariupol on his own. As well as our grandfather, we didn't know where my aunt and my cousin were. We heard only fleeting rumors about which building they were hiding in but had no address or other information. I just kept praying for the rest of our family in Mariupol, for my boyfriend, and for the future of each of us. My father went to Mariupol, but he could not get to our neighborhood, as there were battles raging. He was about to walk. He wanted to continue on foot. My father had left eight years ago and had never seen how beautiful the city had become. Now he found it destroyed. Dad came to the village and found the house, but the doors were locked. Suddenly I received a message on Viber from my mother's sister saying that she was in a village not far from Mariupol. I immediately gave this information to my father, and he went there. Dad came to the village and found the house, but the doors were locked.

Realizing that he needed to stay overnight somewhere, he was about to go to a local refugee reception center when suddenly the gates of the house opened, and his grandfather (father of my mother), aunt (sister of my mother), and sister (my cousin) came out. These were the circumstances under which they met for the first time in eight years. As it turned out, my aunt and sister had been in the basement of some relatives for about a month and could not leave because of the heavy shelling. They eventually risked leaving on foot, arriving at a house outside Mariupol. When they got there, the mother of my cousin's father met them and saw our grandfather there, who had come on foot two days earlier. The miracle is that we all understood that we needed to get out, and did it alone, went through the many dangers, and were able to survive. The most incredible thing is that my father was able to get to Mariupol and find them, and they all met together under such difficult and dangerous circumstances.

This story remains unfinished because the war is not over yet. How many more lives will it destroy and how many cities will be destroyed before it can be stopped? It will take time for this to happen and peace not only in the Universe but also in our hearts. I say thanks to the Universe for every day I live here because the war is still going on, people are still dying, and I continue to live.

I understood and realized an exceedingly important thought that helped me to keep my mind strong: "You cannot control everything that happens to you. But you can control how you react. Your strength is in your fight."

[Author's note: Kristina's boyfriend Pavlo was imprisoned and tortured by the Russian army. He was released on November 3, 2022. Kristina and Pavlo were married on April 24, 2023].

By Anastasia Selevanova

Date of birth: April 24, 2012
From: Mariupol
Position: A schoolgirl who wants to be an artist
In Mariupol at the start of the invasion; escaped with her cousin and her aunt to Gdansk, Poland

July 26, 2022

February 24 was supposed to be a day like any other, with nothing to foretell misfortune. Everything was sudden. I woke up to the noise and bustle of the house. My cousin had thrown everything into her backpack, and my aunt, who was supposed to be at work, was at home. She said she hadn't made it to work, that she'd heard the explosions and had immediately run to us. We didn't know what was going on, everyone was sitting in front of the TV and reading the news on their cell phones. On TV, they were saying that we should stay at home, where it was safest: in the hallway, the bathroom, or the cellar. It all seemed like a bad dream. During the explosions, we sat in the little hallway—me, my cousin, my aunt, my grandmother, my great-grandmother, and our cat, Chorik. My aunt told us to sleep on the floor with our clothes on. Because of the Russian attack, there was no electricity, no gas, no water. Later, when we could still hear the explosions, we ran into the cellar, where we stayed for about a month. It was hell . . . There was hardly anything to eat, and we made soup over the fire with water extracted from the radiators. The children were all infected with the rotavirus one after the other. Despite these circumstances, the soup tasted good. We didn't go out because of the constant bombing. We all looked pale yellow and dirty. Artem, Veronika, and I held out and even played games, sang songs, painted, read by candlelight, and looked at photos on our cell phone when it was still charged.

When it became clear that we weren't going to be rescued because the Orcs wouldn't let the evacuation buses through, people started leaving by car when they could. We didn't have a car, so all we could do was sit and wait for everything to pass. Besides us, there was only one other family who didn't have a car either. We were hopeless.

One morning, we woke up to a voice saying: "I'm going to take someone with children to Zaporizhzhia." My aunt ran off and agreed with the man that he would take us where we had acquaintances we could stay with. Within five minutes, we were packed. Me, my cousin and my aunt got into the car. I didn't even have time to hug my grandmother—she couldn't leave my ninety-two-year-old great-grandmother—nor did I have time to say goodbye to our cat Chorik. I never saw him again; he burned down along with my grandmother's house. We arrived in the evening, having driven under fire and passed eighteen Russian checkpoints. Each time, I was afraid they wouldn't let us through. On several occasions, our savior encouraged and reassured us. It wasn't until we got close to Vasylivka, where we were escorted by Ukrainian police, that we could breathe. Our savior's name was Vladislav, and he wanted

to go and find his parents, but he couldn't reach them, so he went to the first shelter along the way and saved us. We nicknamed him "Angel." We stayed in Zaporizhzhia for a few days, but as there was nowhere safe in Ukraine, we left for Poland.

Everything's fine now. We're safe. There's a sea here, like at home in Mariupol, but I'd love to see my Mariupol sea. What's more, they deprived me of the chance to visit my mother at the cemetery, who died two years ago . . .

[Author's note: Little Nastia has everything a child needs in Poland: an apartment where she lives with her aunt and cousin, a school she likes, friends to play with, peace and security. At night, there are no sirens wailing and bombs falling. Viktoria, her aunt, says that Nastia seems very happy, but is desperate to go home and return to Mariupol. The challenge for Viktoria is to make her niece understand that this is not possible as the city has been destroyed and is under Russian occupation.]

By Oksana L.

Date of birth: February 14, 1986
From: Kyiv
Profession: Teacher, actress, night-club manager
In Sri Lanka at the start of the invasion; returned to Ukraine in March 2022

July 29, 2022

Every morning, I send a message to my mother: "Everything's fine, I'm safe," but that's not quite true. There are no front lines here. Here, in Kramatorsk, Bakhmut, Sloviansk, Lyssychansk, and Druzhkivka, war is everywhere. You hear it, you see it, you talk about it. The sale of alcohol is forbidden. There are very few natives left.

When we checked into the hotel, I asked if there were any military or strategic installations nearby. "There's military everywhere here," replied receptionist Sasha. And it was true. The hotel has an ATM (one of two in the city), and there's always a line of soldiers out front. Policemen live in the hotel: they rest, make noise at night, and sometimes they want to talk. Upstairs, wires and plywood hang from the ceiling. A missile fell not far from here.

I order apple pie and pancakes for breakfast. It was my last breakfast of this trip in this hotel. They cook with love here, but there aren't enough vegetables. F. and I have always lacked vegetables, as we don't eat meat, and in this hotel, there is only one salad: tomatoes with cucumbers and dill. We always order a double portion. I am sitting at a wooden table in the dining room. I arrived very early. I don't want to talk to anyone. I drink coffee and wait for my pancakes.

After breakfast, we had to load F.'s belongings and set off for Dnipro, then Kyiv. Yesterday, the two of us packed our things. I picked up the laundry from the hotel. "It's still a bit wet," said Tania, the receptionist. She didn't ask me for any money for the laundry. We put F.'s laundry, washing bag, basin, cereal bars, papers, a complete folder with first-aid instructions, and clothes in her backpack. I remove the shower gel because there's not enough room. We put the electronics, charger, and computer in a separate bag.

F.'s camera, the blood-stained camera, is in the car on the back seat. That is where I used to sit most of the time, but now I am sitting in the front. Someone gave me the camera at the Lyssychansk police station. I don't know if it was a policeman. When I took the camera in my hand, it was still filming. I saw blood and bits of I don't know what on my hands. I got scared, looked at my hands and said: "There are pieces . . . There are pieces here!" Someone came up to me and wiped my hands with his, and a stern man made me wash my hands with soap, even though I didn't want to. I was given a pill. I'll never lose control of myself again.

That evening, at the hotel, I called a soldier I knew to ask him if we had been able to save F. He told me he had seen the photos, the uncensored, unretouched photos. There was no chance. I asked him to send me the photos. So he did. Later, I would look at the photos, and the video from F.'s camera, I would claim the right to see the body through the embassy, acquaintances at the morgue,

and the administration. No success. I will offer my services as an interpreter at the autopsy, as I already have experience in this field. I am turned down because of a conflict of interest. After the autopsy, I will call the prosecutor's office and ask again if we could have saved F. "They removed half a kilo of iron, he died in forty seconds, he lost two liters of blood, a splinter went through his tongue and lodged in his brain. They couldn't have saved him." I will write to a coroner I know and invite him for coffee when I get back to Kyiv.

In the hotel near Kramatorsk, journalists form a semicircle around us. I am not crying, I think the receptionist Marina said we had to pay a thousand hryvnia for each lost key, and we have already lost two.

[Author's note: F. is a French reporter, who was killed in the line of duty. Oksana continues to work as fixer and is involved in two theater projects: one in Ukraine and the other one in France.]

By Olha Olshanska

Date of birth: October 1, 1986
From: Kyiv
Profession: Project manager with the NGO Insight
First encounter with war: 2014, while coordinating the Shelter project to support LGBTQIA+ people who have left the occupied territories and Crimea.
In Kyiv at the start of the invasion; departed for Budapest on March 1, 2022. Travelled to Berlin on March 3, 2022. Returned to Kyiv in August 2022.

November 5, 2022

My name is Olha. I'm a lesbian, feminist, and human rights activist. I've spent a large part of my life campaigning for a tolerant and open society, free of stereotypes and prejudice, in our country, and fighting discrimination. I realized quite early, at the age of fourteen, that I was a lesbian, and as I've never suffered from homophobia in my environment, I consider it more of a bonus and a privilege. I naturally accept myself and don't consider myself special because of my orientation, so I'd like society to treat me accordingly. Loving someone of the same sex doesn't mean having sex all the time or participating in orgies, as the majority of our society stereotypically thinks. We are the same people and live the same life as everyone else in our country. Unfortunately, our society is still rather hard on this community, and it remains a very vulnerable group in our country, deprived of many fundamental rights.

The organization I work for was founded in 2008 by a group of like-minded people from the LGBTQIA+ community. We simply wanted to change our country for the better and help the community.

With this letter, I also want to draw attention to the fact that for us, as for everyone else in Ukraine, the war began in 2014. We too were on the Maidan from the start, working as volunteers and helping our people; no one could stay on the sidelines. Profound changes were taking place in our country.

In June 2014, *Insight* launched the *Shelter* project for LGBTQIA+ people who had to flee the occupied territories of Luhans'k, Donets'k, and Crimea. I remember all the stories of the people who were with us during *Shelter*'s five years of existence, all the stories of war, destroyed lives, despair due to loss, stories of having to start a new life in an unknown place, without family, without a home. As an empathetic person, I felt compassion for all these people. It's a very difficult task to help people, especially those who are traumatized.

Maybe I'm too optimistic, or maybe it was just an inner need to conceal reality, not wanting to admit that such a thing could happen, so that neither I, nor my family, nor my colleagues were prepared for a full-scale invasion.

I remember February 23 very well. It was a Wednesday. I finished my usual day's work at the office, went out, and decided to take a walk. I strolled through the old town, took the funicular up to the park, went for a coffee, and spent all my time on the phone. First with our coordinator in Zaporizhzhia, Natalia, and then with a volunteer in L'viv. We talked about new ideas and plans for a future joint project. I was very inspired and, as always, I already had a clear idea of what I was going to do in a month's time, in six months' time, and by the end of the year. Then I went to a store, bought some sweets for dinner the next day, went to my partner's studio to pick her up from work, and we went together to the

Musafir restaurant (Crimean Tatar cuisine) on the next street. I remember we ate plov, tchebourek, and sweets, and drank deliciously flavored coffee. It was my last wonderful evening in my peaceful Kyiv, in my home, in my peaceful life, and I had no idea that it would be the last day of my normal life.

Since I was a teenager, I've traveled extensively, visiting thirty-six countries and many cities, taking with me many interesting and wonderful memories. I've always felt, and said, that home was wherever I was. Whether it was a hotel in Paris or an inn in Naples, I felt that everything we had was inside us and that my home was me. So I had to flee my home in Kyiv out of fear for my life and that of my family, because it became clear that you only appreciate something familiar when you lose it, something that could never seem to disappear.

The feeling of security was gone, cold, sticky fear had set in, helplessness, despair, sadness, suffering, depression. All these feelings invaded me from within and paralyzed my body.

Around five o'clock on February 24, 2022, I woke up to the sound of missiles. My work chats were immediately filled with messages. I coordinated the work of the regional delegations, we had ten all over the country at the time, of which I was very proud, and there were also our colleagues in Kyiv, all writing, asking if we were still alive, trying to support each other. They were giving us advice on what to do, how to glue the windows so that they would break into bigger pieces and the shards wouldn't hurt us . . . I thought I was going to open my eyes and wake up, and that it was all just a nightmare that was now over.

My partner went to get water, medicine, and so on . . . She found it interesting to be among people and try to understand what was going on. That's her protective mechanism. And what did I do? I put blankets in the hallway between two walls and spent the next five days there. I couldn't eat, I drank a lot of water, I got up sometimes and spent my time reading the news and communicating with my relatives all over the country. During those days, I lost seven kilos due to stress, which I regained when I was safe in Berlin and chaotically mixed everything up: cold supermarket sandwiches or fast food.

After just a few days, it was clear that our organization needed to reorganize all its work. Community members asked us to help them get to western Ukraine and further into the EU. When you're standing in the hallway waiting for a missile to hit your house, it's very difficult to help others at the same time. So I decided to go somewhere safe. I wrote to my friend and colleague, who had been living in Berlin for two years, to ask if he could put me up in his house for two weeks with my partner and the cat. He immediately replied that they were expecting us and would lend us their room. Generally speaking, a lot of people from abroad wrote to me at the time to support me, express their compassion, and offer their help, which I really appreciate and will be grateful for the rest of my life. People are the most important thing in life. Not just anything. Just people and relationships.

We were packed and ready in forty minutes. We didn't have a carrier for the cat, we simply put it in a sports bag. We took a change of linen and some important documents. It was already impossible to get from the left bank to the main station.

We were lucky enough to have friends who lived nearby and who took us by car to the Darnytsia station, from where a daily train was due to leave for Lviv. What followed was a nightmare I'll probably remember for the rest of my life.

We stood on the station platform waiting for the train. As time went by, more and more people arrived with suitcases, small children, elderly people, and animals. Many of them had three, or five cats, and several dogs, some had parrots.

What seemed like a nightmare was reality on March 1, 2022.

There were no announcements about which track the train would be arriving on, although there were a few people in uniform, but no one was regulating anything. From time to time, people would simply get up and run to another track, no one knowing exactly where the train was going to arrive.

So we waited for an hour. The train arrived on the next platform and the whole crowd rushed in, some throwing their suitcases and losing their belongings en route. There was a lot of shouting and noise. Everyone was running to get on the train as fast as possible, pushing everything and everyone aside. We ran, but the train was already almost full. I realized that we wouldn't be able to get in, and I was really afraid of hurting our cat. It was the most precious thing I had at the time.

People were packed into the train like sardines. The risk of injury was very high. Once, I turned my head and heard a scream so piercing and desperate that I could still hear it in my head six months later... Stronger men than him pushed everyone back so they could get on the train, and nothing stopped them. And that scream belonged to a woman whose husband had snatched her baby from her and boarded the train when the doors closed. The woman remained on the platform... The tears came to my eyes, it was unbearable, there was so much pain... It was really a matter of survival.

I told my partner that we shouldn't get involved and that we should be on our guard. There might be another train. I started googling. My friends wrote that another train was leaving for Lviv in about half an hour. So we stood there waiting. We didn't know if we were going to be able to get there, we didn't have a car and it was pretty dangerous to drive there. All the channels were reporting that whole families had been shot dead in their cars, and I thought that at that point the train would be the safest way for us to get there.

After half an hour, another train arrived marked Kharkiv-Kyiv. It was a fast train, and once again the crowds were pouring in, including us.

It really was our last chance.

We were able to board. There were already a lot of people inside, a lot of young people, probably from Ukraine, and foreign students. They were fleeing Kharkiv. We asked where the train was going, but everyone was silent, nobody said anything, and the sign always said Kharkiv-Kyiv. In my confusion, I thought the train was going to Kharkiv, which was being razed to the ground, but five minutes later the sign said Kyiv-L'viv, and I felt a little better. Most of the people waiting on the platform got on this train. Women of all ages and children. Some men with wives and babies, and large families. People tried to get the young men to stand up so the older women could sit down, but they weren't very sympathetic. They even pusillanimously replied that they had finally bought a ticket . . . We didn't have tickets, and no one controlled them in this situation. The train actually had a capacity of 579 people. According to rough estimates, the car inspector said that four thousand people were traveling at the same time on the train. There wasn't a single empty seat. I stayed in the same position and we traveled for twelve hours. It was very tiring. All in all, it was a very hard day and experience, and everything that happened afterward seemed to be just a continuation of hell.

We arrived overnight in L'viv, where we spent the next two nights at our friend Dana's house, and during the day we looked for transport, but there was none. We also had to get the cat microchipped and sort out a few other details. In L'viv, I was startled every time a streetcar went by. The loud, shrill noises still scare me today, like the aerial alarm. We're all united by trauma.

After two days, we continued across the Hungarian border to Záhony, where women from the *Budapest Pride* organization picked us up and took us to a couple's house for the night. We stayed there for two more days. The most important thing was to finally buy a carrier for the cat, who was running out of air in the bag and struggling. In one of the shopping centers, we found a pet shop . . . I remember walking into the mall and seeing normal life take its course. It smelled of pastries, people were shopping, and some had flowers. They were taking a leisurely stroll, drinking coffee—all this, too, we'd had just a few days before. Now my country is being torn apart, destroyed, civilian objects are being bombarded with cruise missiles, people are being raped and murdered. That's when my mother started writing goodbye notes on Messenger. I was completely devastated. I stood there crying in the middle of this other foreign life in a residential area of Budapest.

A few days later, we arrived in Berlin, and I was finally able to fully immerse myself in working remotely. We lost our office in Odesa, then our coordinator left Kramatorsk, and our wonderful, beloved office was closed, along with the one in Zaporizhzhia. We opened housing for LGBTQIA+ people in Chernivtsi and L'viv, a humanitarian center in L'viv to help women and children. Some of our colleagues stayed in Kyiv, but most left for safer places in western Ukraine and abroad.

For six months, I was in charge of finding relocation opportunities for the community. I gave advice and responded to requests from people leaving for western Ukraine, as many people in the community were fleeing to the EU.

In six months, we changed apartments three times. First, we lived with my friend for two weeks, as agreed, in the boys' room. Then we were lucky enough to meet a local family, Misha and Dasha, and their two children. They offered us the office in their apartment. We slept on a mattress on the floor, my first experience of this kind. But we were surrounded by care, and that was the most important thing. Strangers who took us in and helped us as much as they could. It was very precious. We lived with them for about a month, maybe a little longer. I tried to establish contacts with local people and organizations, to take part in anything that could be useful to Ukraine, to talk about the situation of the community, its needs, and the type of help needed in Ukraine. We organized humanitarian aid and managed to send crates of food and toiletries to L'viv twice. At the very least, I wanted to do something useful. Thanks to our contacts with the locals, we found an apartment to rent and moved in for a few months, a small studio where the three of us lived with our cat. We even bought new sheets, a couple of cups, and some plates to feel like we had a home, a temporary home. I was in Kyiv all the time in my head. There was a time when all I could do was stay in bed without getting up when I couldn't see the point of anything, when I didn't feel like I was living my life, and when I only had one question on my mind: why all this? Why was your wonderful life stolen, your home, your bed, your books, your paintings, your clothes, your favorite job, your favorite routes, your places, your people, your plans and hopes, your dreams and goals? It's all gone, and you don't know what to do next, or what's going to happen tomorrow, you can't plan anything because you don't know whether a missile will hit your house in Kyiv and whether you'll have a place to go back to or not . . .

All these thoughts eat you up inside. I consider my life at that time as a simple existence. Eat to live, drink water to live, and go somewhere to distract myself, but nothing helped. A friend recommended a psychologist, whom I consulted. I went once a week to the cemetery near the apartment and we held our session there by video. I did this five times and realized that it wasn't helping me, but making things more difficult. That I didn't have the resources right now. And so I took this time to be alone with my feelings. It was around this time that I decided to go to Kyiv for a week, to see what it was like and decide what to do next. The way back was the most beautiful. I wanted to cry all the time and, when we arrived at the Kyiv station, I simply kissed the ground, so familiar was everything to me.

And above all, I finally felt happy, because this is my home, my country, my city, and this is where I belong. After a week, we went back to Berlin, there were a few bureaucratic matters to sort out, and then we packed up and headed back to Kyiv.

- Am I afraid to live here, in a country at war?
- Am I afraid of being in a city where dozens of missiles are being fired at us and we don't know when or where the next missile will hit?
- Am I afraid of an air raid when I'm on the move and there's no shelter nearby?

No, I'm not. I'm not afraid. This is my home and I'm happy. If it's my destiny to die here, then so be it.

I've had enough opportunities to leave Ukraine, to emigrate, or simply to stay in Germany or choose another country, I've had many offers from friends and acquaintances, but I can't and I don't want to.

I'm happy where I am, and I'll be here as long as my heart beats happily. The most precious thing I've received since this large-scale invasion began has been the encounters with incredible people.

The names of these people are forever engraved in my heart: Katia and Natacha, Oksana and her husband, Dana, Oksana, Vitalina, Viktoria, Marko and his friend, Misha and Misha, Zlata, Indira, Olesia, Misha and Dasha and Nestor, Yasha, Johann and Andreas, Karl, Leila, Anja and the girls, Olena, Veronika, Julia, Natacha. You are incredible people and I will never forget your kindness, support, and care.

By Maryna Kamenskaya

Date of birth: September 26, 1979
From: Luts'k
Profession: Art therapist
In Luts'k at the start of the invasion; escaped with her daughter, Valeria (fifteen at the time), on March 6, 2022, to Lublin, Poland. Both returned to Luts'k in early August 2022.

August 5, 2022

I begin my letter with the background. On February 23, 2022, my heart was out of place all day long. There were very unsettling feelings in the air that were hard to put into words. There was literally not enough air to breathe. Worry and uncertainty paralyzed me and prevented me from thinking clearly. Anguish froze my body. The night of February 23 to 24 was the worst. The silence was such that you could hear your own heartbeat. Towards morning, I was finally able to fall asleep. At four in the morning, the fighter planes took off. Very, very low, and very loud. I didn't know they were ours yet, and my heart was beating somewhere near my neck. After a few minutes, everything calmed down and there was a great silence. I remember every minute of that night.

Around five in the morning, I received a call from my sister in Kyiv. In view of the imminent danger, she wanted to fly to Spain with her child first thing in the morning. My sister told me that no one was allowed to enter Boryspil airport at the moment and that flight check-in was suspended for half an hour. I ask her to keep me informed. Sleep is out of the question. My fear increases more and more. After twenty minutes, my sister called me and I heard the most terrible news of my life: "Marina, the war has started. Martial law is in force. Kyiv is being bombed."

I get hysterical. My daughter wakes up. I realize I must control myself. But my body and my feelings won't let me. I call my friend: "Olia, it's war." We cry together. My head is in chaos. I don't know what to do or where to run to save my child. Half past five in the morning. Outside, daylight is beginning to break. My daughter and I sit in front of the computer, reading and opening each new message. Something flashes to the right of the window. We looked at each other, wondering what it was. A few seconds later, the terrible sound of an explosion. Valeria runs into her room and huddles in a corner, sobbing loudly. For some reason, I'm in a hurry to close the balcony door. My body is shaking so badly that nothing can calm it. I call my mother. She has a heart condition and I put off calling her until the last moment. But in Luts'k, there are explosions and there's no time to lose. "Mama, the war has started. Kyiv is being bombed, there are explosions in Luts'k. Missiles are flying all over Ukraine." A few minutes later, the explosions were already at home, near L'viv. A terrible, terrible morning. I understand that from now on, there is no safety anywhere.

In a single minute, a man full of complexes gave a criminal order and changed the lives of millions, bringing pain and death. My body continues to tense. To make a phone call, my daughter presses my hand with the phone against my ear. My hands tremble so much I can't hold the receiver. My soul is aching. Everything in me is torn apart. My soul is paralyzed with fear and helplessness.

Another explosion. A sound I'll never forget. Another explosion. And another. Seven missiles flew into my dear, peaceful city on that terrible morning. We remember the sound of each one. I remember my husband's eyes, wanting to help us, to protect us, and his despair and helplessness at the sound of the missiles flying. We understood everything. The street in front of our house was instantly filled with cars. People were fleeing the war.

Oh, my God, I'd never have believed that you could pack a suitcase not with joy for the sea and the sun, but with hands that don't obey you and eyes full of tears. To simply leave, to take your child somewhere. Just to survive, just for your daughter to survive.

By this time, my sister and her family were already in a fallout shelter in Kyiv, waiting for a car to L'viv. After that, they spent almost two interminable days driving at a snail's pace on secondary roads towards western Ukraine. The main road was already mercilessly bombed by the enemy. Arriving in L'viv, they tried to get the children into Poland. The queue at the border was endless.

My sister and I agreed that she would take my Valeria with her. I have an old grandmother I couldn't leave behind. After queuing for two days at the border, my sister had to return to L'viv. The queue had barely moved. A few days later, they arrived in Lublin, Poland, via Hungary. And so the Ukrainians began their terrible journey to Europe.

On March 5, I decided to take my daughter alone to my sister's, via a pedestrian border crossing. By bus, it just wasn't realistic. My husband took us to the Ukrainian side of the border, and words cannot describe what happened there. You can only see and feel it. The icy wind penetrated every cell of our bodies. Hundreds of people, women with infants, exhausted elderly ladies. A young woman nursing a two-week-old baby, people protected her from the wind with jackets. A woman came up to me and told me that her two apartments in Kharkiv no longer existed, that all she had left was this suitcase and her life. An old woman who hugged her dog for warmth. Later, on the Polish side, I wrapped this woman in a blanket. And the men's tears.

It's so horrible to see families separated. That pain in the eyes. Everyone understood everything without words. Then we set off without our men into the unknown. At the Polish border, a huge number of volunteers were waiting for us with all kinds of foodstuffs. There were really all the little things that people might need. And if something was missing, we had the feeling it would be organized immediately. Untiring as bees, the Polish volunteers were hard at work welcoming the Ukrainian women and children.

The cars and buses for the rest of the journey could not cope with the uninterrupted flow of refugees. But the Poles did their best. It was their destiny to be the first to help the Ukrainians. And we are grateful to all the countries in the world that opened their doors and helped. And I carry Poland forever in my heart, like an invisible tattoo. After the border check, a Pole was waiting for us and offered to take us to the town of Zamość and put us on a bus to Lublin. As places on the buses were first allocated to women with babies, we couldn't get past the border control. This kind-hearted man then decided to pick us up directly at the border. But how were we going to find each other? Luckily, we had a bright yellow suitcase. We managed to find our way through the crowd of thousands.

We were so cold we could hardly speak. While we waited for Przemek, we lined up for a hot drink. It didn't matter. The main thing is to be warm. Warming the soul was impossible. At least we warmed the body. After picking us up, Przemek turned up the heat in the car and gave us something to eat. After five minutes, we felt as if we'd known each other for a hundred years. We drove fifty kilometers to the bus station, listening to Ukrainian songs. The tears flowed uninterrupted. My soul was overwhelmed with gratitude. In the evening, we arrived in Lublin, where we once again witnessed the incredible hospitality of the Polish people. At the bus station, volunteers immediately offered their help, and simple folk brought food, water, and clothes to the volunteer center. Once again, there were tears, once again overwhelming gratitude, and love. In Lublin, we were well received by Mrs. Bożena and Mr. Stanisław. They made a whole floor of their house available to us, let us know we could stay as long as we wanted, and gave us all the help we could. Wonderful people with a great soul. It was March 6, 2022, and that day has become a date I'll never forget. Through it all, my fifteen-year-old daughter had bravely endured the cold, the queues, and the pain. My little girl had grown up in a day. Do children have to grow up like that? No, of course not.

That night, we hugged each other tightly and slept for the first time in a week. Sleep was what we had missed so much at home. Every noise, every rustle frightened us to the point of panic. And then, at last, we were able to sleep. Then I had to sort out the legal formalities for my daughter's stay in Poland, and my sister became her temporary guardian. I couldn't stay in Poland. In Luts'k, my grandmother needed care. To ensure that the children didn't lose a school year, Poland immediately set up Ukrainian classes, made the most of the existing situation, and ensured that our children's stay was as pleasant as possible in this difficult situation.

The courses were accompanied by psychological and medical support and interpreters, as well as various excursions and gifts. Valeria immediately found her place. The children, who had to grow up so quickly, stuck together, formed

friendships, and supported each other in difficult times. Four days later, I separated from my child for the first time in my life and returned to Luts'k. Thus began our life in two countries. To say it was painful would be an understatement. The only thought that kept me afloat was that my daughter was safe. Valeria wrote to me every day to tell me about her impressions, her feelings, and the school. It was heartbreaking to see my child only through a video connection and not be able to take her in my arms, hold her close, and give her all the motherly love I could. But knowing she was safe always saved me.

When I arrived in Luts'k, I heard new explosions in the morning. People were being killed. And I realized that she was right to be far away now. March was a month of trials for both of us. Emotionally, we experienced fear, anger, aggression, and infinite love for each other. We felt the importance of life and of every moment. It was very interesting to see how Valeria developed, made new friends in Poland, and learned to live almost independently. To everyone's surprise, in Lublin, she met people her own age whom she had only met at home via the Internet. It was so touching. It was also there that my daughter fell in love for the first time. She spoke to me with such sincerity about her experiences. She felt very much at home in Poland. The one thing that ran through her five-month stay was a strong desire to return home to Ukraine. "I want to go home, Mom. I really want to go home." Be patient, darling, be patient. Just a little longer . . . Just a little longer . . . Month after month, I promised things I had no influence over.

At that time, her life was unfolding in a most interesting way. It was as if the whole universe was helping my child to live harmoniously through this terrible period. I'm very happy that the Poles have managed to organize children's free time in such a way as to protect them as much as possible from psychological trauma. During her stay in Lublin, she saw every corner of the city, attended concerts organized for the occasion, went on excursions to the suburbs and other cities, visited museums, and so on. It means a lot to me that Valeria was able to live through this period without fear or worry. But there were always those incessant "Mom, I'm fine here. But I want to go home."

In Ukraine, it was very difficult to fully grasp the horror of what happened here. The brain and soul are frozen. It's very difficult to switch on your mind and pull yourself together. Every noise, every rustle scares you so much that your knees tremble. The days and nights flew by, in constant anguish and anticipation of the war's imminent end. Each day brought its share of sad news that my mind would neither accept nor understand. For the first month and a half, I was panic-stricken at the thought of leaving the house to go shopping or to the chemist. At home, I felt safe, but outside, I felt totally helpless. It's very scary not to be able to control your emotional state. You can't help but panic when that feeling of panic comes over you. All the bad things I'd experienced up until then didn't seem so bad anymore.

To distract myself from this constant anxiety, I joined the volunteers. Day after day, I concentrated entirely on this activity and tried to communicate as much as possible with people to improve my condition at least a little. While I was still able to manage my emotions during the day, the anxiety increased more and more towards evening. Night time. The most difficult time was at night. As night fell, the city sank into an ominous silence. Not the kind of silence that offers tranquility in the face of city noise, but rather the silence that brings the unknown. This silence was regularly broken, several times a night, by the wail of sirens. Oh, my God, how heartbreaking that noise is. And how the panic filled every cell of my body and every fiber of my soul. My mother and friends had similar feelings.

In spite of everything, we continued to live and help each other emotionally as best we could. Some of us continued to go to work, others quit their jobs to volunteer in the city, and still others did housework. My husband always took me to the park. It was my favorite park, my place of strength in Luts'k. There I could clear my head for a while. And then it would all come back. And so it went on. This period was also one of intense aggression and anger. It bubbled up and covered all the other feelings that wanted to get out. Talking to my friends, I discovered a number of things they had in common, such as the fear of distracting themselves, even with a film. Everyone was focused on the war. I understood one thing with great clarity: the war made us understand the special value of life. And it made us realize that nothing would ever be the same again. The process of adapting to new realities had begun.

For me, April was the month I accepted the war. As soon as I understood what the war entailed, my inner revolt disappeared. I realized that all the emotions linked to this process were natural and normal. This is what happened when I returned from Poland in the second half of April. I saw the Ukrainian border and realized that I had to either accept the new living conditions or leave the country. There was no other solution. And I was seized with a love so incredible that I had only one thought: "Ukraine is my homeland. I'm going to live in this new reality." Another month passed, and then another . . . The news portals were filled with all kinds of information. Ukraine was being destroyed a little more every day. My daughter and I learned to combine seemingly incompatible emotions: pain, fear, aggression, and the unrealistic desire to live and appreciate every moment, to love. The value of life is no longer just a word. It is a way of life, its quality. At such a terrible price.

It's July. My sister has decided to move to Sweden. I'm grateful to her for these five difficult months during which my Valeria has lived in safety. On July 17, I left for Poland and, for the first time, came home with my daughter. As I write these lines, we are still in Lublin. We've spent three wonderful weeks here. We've been to Warsaw, learned about the history of the Majdanek concentration camp, and walked over a hundred kilometers through the city. And we're glad God gave us this time. We're happy to be able to walk through the old streets holding hands for the tenth time in a week. We drink coffee together, eat ice cream and unhealthy fast food. Because it's not the number of calories ingested that counts. What matters is that we have this moment, this time, and this opportunity. It's the most precious thing in the world.

Three days later, on August 5, exactly five months after crossing the border on a freezing spring day, I can say to my Valeria for the first time, "Honey, we're coming home." I can't promise her safety, I can't stop the war, but I can teach her to live in this new reality. I can wrap her in my infinite love and surround her with motherly protection. And we both believe that we will overcome this difficult ordeal. God willing, every Ukrainian, in every corner of the world, will soon hear the news of the end of the war and Ukraine's victory. And everyone will return to rebuild the country and create a happy future for the most precious people in the world: our children. Everything will be new, and it will be difficult. But the most important thing is that we will once again be able to see the peaceful skies above our homeland, Ukraine. I'm grateful for the opportunity to take part in this project. It means a lot to me.

[Author's note: Valeria has finished school, is studying graphic design and works as a waitress in a café. Marina is dedicated to supporting women in nurturing their psychological well-being through the medium of art therapy. She regularly visits her sister in Gothenburg, Sweden].

By Kateryna Vozianova

Date of birth: April 10, 1983
From: Kyiv
Profession: Founder of the Indposhiv, Heroism, and Mozart Street brands
In Kyiv at the start of the invasion; left the capital with her husband and children on the same day for Western Ukraine, returning to Kyiv on April 28, 2022.

August 10, 2022

I'm lying on the bed. It's 4:30 a.m. and I have to pack for a business trip to Odesa. My team and I go there every month. It's my second favorite city. After Kyiv. As before every business trip, I have a slight feeling of apprehension. I'm a bit afraid of being separated from my children (I have two, Yeva is six and Kai will soon be two). What's more, the subject of war has been in the air for over a month, but CNN's predictions of an invasion on February 16 have not come true. So there will be no war.

I start my day calmly. February 24th. The day that, as I'm about to find out in half an hour, is going to change my whole life. I take a shower and go back to bed to look at some Instagram posts. This is how I prefer to spend my morning, without haste. And then I hear an explosion. A violent explosion, certainly not a muffler or a firework. Shortly afterward, a second explosion. First, I wake up my husband. He tells me not to worry and to keep sleeping. The social media went wild: explosions in Kyiv, in Kharkiv. Explosions all over Ukraine. All the Telegram chats are going off. It's hard to believe, but it's already obvious: war has begun.

Until the last moment, I didn't believe it would happen. How could a real war take place in Europe in the twenty-first century? A few days earlier, I had gathered my entire Indposhiv team to reassure everyone. Before the war, I had a wonderful business making men's tailored suits. We had seventy-three employees, the business was growing, and we had millions of projects. I got all my staff together and told them there were three possible scenarios for how things would evolve. I gave the most pessimistic scenario (a full-scale war) a maximum probability of 5%. Can anyone imagine tanks on the streets of Kyiv? Kyiv is my favorite city in the world. I've had several opportunities to go to Europe or the United States, but I've always chosen to stay here.

That morning, we decided to leave Kyiv. In the space of half an hour, we woke up the children and the nanny, packed a bag with the bare necessities (in my case, three black dresses—I don't wear pants), and headed for the car. I think I remember every second of that day. I remember waking Yeva up and telling her that she didn't have to go to school that day and that we were going on a little excursion. I remember waking up the nanny and telling her to get her and Kai's things ready. Diapers, food, clothes. She asks me for how long. I replied that it was for three days. Although I realize it won't be three. So I correct her: "For a week." Later, she told me she didn't believe me when I said the war had started. I was far too calm.

I remember closing the apartment with the feeling that we might never come back. It's a terribly oppressive feeling. When I closed the door, I realized that at that moment, I was closing a very happy chapter in my life. A thirty-eight-year chapter in which EVERY year was better than the last. A chapter in which I'd had a great career, which I was now ending when my company was at its peak. A chapter in which my classmate finally became my husband. A chapter in which we worked hard and managed to buy a car, then an apartment, then a house in the country. A chapter in which I woke up almost every morning feeling like the happiest person in the world. I thanked life every day and was sure that the best was yet to come. I closed that chapter and opened another. A chapter where bombs are being dropped on our city. Where tanks roam the streets, where unarmed people are shot. A chapter where people live in subway stations, children are born in cellars, and the elderly die without medicine. At the time, I wanted the memory of this past chapter to be erased. So that I could never compare the past with the present. Because if I do, I would want to die.

We didn't know where we were going. We weren't going somewhere, we were leaving somewhere.

By six o'clock in the morning, the whole city was already jammed. It seemed like everyone with a car was really driving. I was worried about the children. Yeva had already realized that our "excursion" had been forced. That we were on the run, that planes were flying overhead and they weren't airliners. We tried to restrain ourselves from saying what we wanted, but that's why the atmosphere in the car was so tense and unnatural.

How do you talk to children about war? How do you explain why it happens and when it ends? How to answer a million questions, from "Where are we going?" to "What about Grandma and Grandpa?"

After two hours of stop-and-go driving, we left Kyiv behind. We drove through the small satellite town of Irpin. Four hours later, there were already tanks and Russian soldiers shooting at civilians.

One important decision I took almost immediately was not to leave Ukraine. It's hard to explain rationally, but inwardly, I had the feeling that my country had become a kind of living man. And this person was now in a very bad way: he was torn apart from the inside, he had wounds on many parts of his body and tumors on others. It's not at all clear what exactly is triggering this, but I can't let this person down. For, as the saying goes, "for better or for worse." What's more, I was 100% sure that the war wouldn't last more than a week. That the whole world would see it now, intervene, and put this mad dictator in his place.

We decided to travel to western Ukraine. The journey took around thirty-four hours. It may sound long and arduous, but it's not. When you read about people carrying mattresses into the cellar or sleeping on the floor in metro stations, you realize that sleeping in a car is a luxury. What surprised me most were our children. I've never seen them so calm and well-behaved. I think that at times like these, all living beings understand at a molecular level what they have to do. Yeva and Kai have understood that they have to sit still, even if it's difficult.

You can't be prepared for war if you've never experienced it. War is illogical, monstrous, uncivilized, and a dead end. The more news you hear about what's going on, the more you begin to form a new idea of the world. And that's precisely what's repugnant, but inevitable. In this world, a man can rape a five-year-old child in front of his mother, a father can be tortured in front of his children. In this world, people are shot in the back, missiles fall on a house where people are sleeping peacefully, and a theater is destroyed while six hundred people are trying to take shelter from the bombs in its basement.

Worst of all, this world isn't any other. It's the same world where people plan vacations, where children go to school, where young people graduate and take entrance exams. It's the same world where there are queues outside Louis Vuitton stores, where people worry about obesity and hair loss. These people simply don't think about war. Just as we didn't think about it before.

After more than twenty-four hours, we arrived at the hotel, the only one in the L'viv region that still had two rooms available. Everything seemed completely surreal. During the night, while the children slept in their seats, my husband Andriy and I planned the itinerary, thinking about how we could get around the airport, as missiles had been launched at all the airports. Fifteen hours earlier, we had no idea where we were going to spend the night, or even where we were going to live. I was seriously afraid that, like many others, we would have to sleep on the floor of a gymnasium in the Khmelnytskyi region. On the first day of the war, money is useless. And now, after spending the previous night in the car, we arrive at a hotel where there is at least the appearance of a peaceful life. People move about unhurriedly, some with cups to drink (Truskavets, the place where we were, is known for its hot springs). Children are running around, the winter sun is shining. Some stores are open, and there's petrol at the filling stations. However, if you listen, you realize that everyone is talking about one thing. The war.

In fact, I love hotels. Before the war, Andriy and I traveled a lot, and choosing a hotel was always my favorite thing to do. That feeling of arriving in another little world where every detail has been thought of, where there are staff who ensure a good atmosphere, who do everything to make you feel good. I hadn't been to a hotel I didn't like for a long time. But this was a completely different situation. The hotel we arrived at wasn't my choice—it was our refuge, our asylum.

I think that's when there were no longer any notions of "comfort zones" or the like. That is, somewhere inside, there was still the old me with its standards of living. It was already clear that all norms were going to hell and new ones were taking their place. The norms of war life.

My mother is a diplomat, she warned me a long time ago that there would be a war. Of course, I dismissed this as an exaggerated fear, as the usual worry of a "mom," even though her daughter will be forty next year. But my mother was right. She didn't want to leave Kyiv under any circumstances. It turned out later that this was a common "problem" with adult parents. You can't even get them away from the frontline hotspots. The telephone connection was regularly interrupted, so my mother and I communicated mainly via Messenger. I've reread our correspondence from that time. As soon as I saw that there was an air alert in Kyiv, I would write to her immediately and tell her to go to the hallway.

During the war, we learned the "two-wall rule." If there's no real air-raid shelter, it's best to follow this rule. According to this rule, you're less likely to be killed by a shockwave if you're behind a second wall, as seen from the street. The first wall (where the windows are usually located) is destroyed and the shards fly against the second wall. This is why many people sit in the hallway during air attacks.

On the whole, at times like these, we don't think so much about the future—because it's totally uncertain—as about the past. Did I make the right decisions at the time? Was I right to stay in Ukraine when I had the option of leaving? Was it right to live "the high life" and buy an apartment, albeit real estate, which, as we can see now, is more of a disadvantage than an advantage? Were we right not to leave Kyiv earlier and hear those explosions? What about the air raid? Was it right to spend all last year's profits on building an extra floor for my company's customers? Was it right to have children in a country where there's a political cataclysm every five to seven years?

I don't tend to feel guilty about things that have gone before, and I don't tend to look back. I only do it to work quickly on mistakes. All my life, my brain, and my attention have been focused on the future. Are you familiar with the advice of all coaches: "Live here and now," i.e. live in the present to be truly happy? I've never understood it, even though I used to consider myself a very happy person. How can you live in the here and now if you're so driven by your plans and dreams? For me, this "here and now" has always been synonymous with short-sightedness and irresponsibility.

The war changed this attitude. Because no matter how much we looked to the future, there was nothing there to hold on to and draw joy from. All projects, all dreams, and all hopes seemed silly to me, the product of a "past life," and this brought me the most terrible feeling: self-pity. In order not to give in to it, I decided not to make plans for the years to come, but for the days to come. Today

I have to go shopping at the supermarket, in the afternoon I have to go for a walk with the kids, until six o'clock I have to decide what I'm going to do with the customer orders that haven't yet been processed, and so on.

During the first weeks of the war, work helped me a lot psychologically. When you're completely disorientated and don't know what to do, the need to make clear decisions at work saves you. We had to make a lot of decisions, from evacuating employees who hadn't managed to leave Kyiv to what to do with the premises. We had just beautifully refurbished our Indposhiv building and turned it into a real gentlemen's club—my dream. Should we nail up the windows with plywood panels so as not to break any glass and prevent looters from breaking in? What should we do with the establishment? Will the security service continue to operate? How can salaries be paid and employees financially supported if the company is at a standstill? How long will it have to shut down?

On February 13, eleven days before the start of the war, my company celebrated its thirteenth anniversary. My company is my pride, my purpose in life, my driving force, and my fulfillment. In its early years, I devoted all my time to it. Many of my colleagues are like family to me. A few days after the start of the war, when personal security issues were largely settled, all those who wanted to leave had left and the others who wanted to stay in Kyiv had adapted to wartime living conditions, with sirens, air attacks, and the constant noise of artillery, I decided to do everything in my power to keep the company going. I wouldn't close it down, I wouldn't sell it and, if possible, I wouldn't downsize either. Because I simply can't imagine living without the company. That's why all the next steps were aimed at maintaining and guaranteeing the ability to work.

I developed a daily routine that kept me from sinking into despair and depression. When we woke up in the morning, we'd have breakfast, then Yeva would start her online courses, Andriy would go to work, I'd help Yeva and the nanny would take Kai for a walk. Then we met up for lunch, and I went to work, either in the lobby of our hotel or—an unimaginable luxury—in a café in the center of Truskavets. Then dinner, news, tea and chocolate, and the night's rest. Each day was identical to the last, which is probably why the days passed so quickly.

And so spring arrived unnoticed. Not calendar spring, but natural spring. I remember walking out of my house and being amazed: the sun was shining, the birds were singing, and people were no longer wrapped up in their scarves. Everyone was looking at each other with a slight smile; it was clear that spring really was a time of hope. And it was clear that everyone had the same hope.

On March 29, Russia announced that it was withdrawing its troops from the Kyiv area. I remember how dizzy I felt when I read this news. Right from the start of the war, I couldn't stop thinking about what victory would be like. How would we find out? What would happen when we heard the news? Would we all weep with joy, men kissing women and children releasing balloons? None of this happened, mainly because no one knew what it meant or whether it would really happen. It wasn't clear whether this was a decoy to get everyone to come back and then strike. Or another short-term maneuver. What decision could be made on the basis of this information? The war had been going on for over a month, a very long time for the modern world, given its intensity.

I remember my feelings as if they were today. A feeling of deep joy. A feeling similar to the one you get when you bring a child into the world. It's like the most beautiful flower in the world is starting to bloom inside you, but you can't tell anyone about it because you're not sure what it is inside you. What if it's just an illusion?

Then we found out about Butsha, and our lives changed irreversibly. From the outside, it may seem that people at war are prepared for anything. But that's not the case. The boundaries of your "everything" naturally expand as you go along, but they also have their limits. Butsha, (it's only a generic term, there were many cities like that) however dissolved the limits of the imaginable. After reading about all these atrocities, violence, and murders, I think I was silent for half a day. I simply couldn't say anything. A friend's family was killed there. Mother, father and son. Only the daughter was still alive. They were found stabbed in a barrel. Not to mention the violence against the children. It was unbearable to see, read, or discuss. This tragedy was so overwhelming that it was clear this wound would not go away, no matter how much time passed, no matter how or when the war ended. It will remain in our hearts.

The amazing thing about war is that its physical proximity has an immediate effect on our perception of its actuality. As soon as there are no more missiles nearby, our bodies seem to protect us and our brains say: don't worry, everything's fine. We can go for a walk, drink wine on the terrace, make plans, and so on. I felt this effect in western Ukraine, where there was almost no impact. But wherever you are, the proximity of suffering to your home is directly proportional to the proximity of suffering to your heart.

Before the war and before Butsha, I never thought evil could be so visible and blatant. After all, we live in a world where every step is visible, at least on Instagram. In theory, these steps made visible to all, are not made visible for the sake of being judged. That means they can't be "bad" a priori. As it turns out, this is not the case. That evil, even in its biblical sense, exists, spreads and, if the public tolerates it, is still encouraged by it. Do you remember the *Matrix* movie, the situation in which Neo realized that the whole world around him was just a simulation? It was the same for me. After Butsha, I realized that the world I'd been living in was very much an illusion. For I stubbornly refused to see the evil that, as it turned out, was right beside me.

I lived with this feeling for two months, and on April 28 we decided to return to Kyiv. It was a spontaneous decision, we suddenly realized that we couldn't stand being away from home any longer. We packed our bags, took the kids, got in the car, and set off for our new life.

During the two months of the war, I cried twice. The first time was when my colleagues sent me a video message on my birthday. I saw in this video how much the people who were so familiar to me had changed. I couldn't help but burst into tears. The second time, I cried when I was interviewed and talked about the incredible people who live in Ukraine and the help and support they give each other on a daily basis. I swore to myself that the third time around, I'd cry with nothing but happiness. And that happiness will be there when I push open the door of our apartment, which I left two months ago thinking it could be forever.

The journey to Kyiv took eight hours, with no traffic jams or delays. Only a few people dared to return at the time. The last leg of the journey took place in Irpin, a town where almost 70% of the houses had been destroyed and burned. It's impossible to convey the emotion that comes over you when you see this. You see the black, burnt houses, the gaping holes in the walls, the bullet and shell marks, and you can't help thinking: this isn't happening to me, not to us. It just can't be. However, the proximity of such a terrible reality gradually changes your consciousness. Probably irreversibly.

We arrived late in the evening at our apartment. I waited for the moment when my body would exhale, relax, and allow itself to cry, but it didn't happen. I simply went back to my apartment, put my things down, and put the kids to bed, which surprised me.

That's when my new life began. All the things from my first life are still there, but I've had to establish a new relationship with them. For example, the bed. Before the war, it was simply a very comfortable bed that my husband and I had chosen, with a perfectly fitting high mattress and beautiful sheets. Now, the bed has become an object of permanent gratitude. Thank you for having it, for sleeping in it. Thank you that it's mine, exactly as I want it. And so it is with many things.

I'm sure the war has made me a different woman. As it seems to me now, a better person. I always thought that my moral values were good and right and that I didn't need to reconsider them. In reconsidering them, albeit at great cost, I've realized that I love myself more after almost six months of war than I did before.

I'm finishing this letter on August 10, in two weeks' time it's Independence Day and, as fate would have it, six months of war. None of us in Ukraine knows what tomorrow will bring—maybe we'll be hit by missiles, maybe Russia will announce its capitulation (in its typical way of presenting it as a "gesture of goodwill"), maybe our government will sign a peace treaty, maybe our allies will finally deliver long-range artillery. I don't know what tomorrow will bring, but I do know what the future will bring.

We have all become part of a monstrous but necessary process: the formation of a new Ukrainian nation. United in our common pain, we finally know exactly what our national identity and national idea are. All my life, I thought it was primitive to be proud of one's nationality—after all, we don't choose it. Now I think the exact opposite. No matter how much pain and suffering we still have to endure, I'm ready. Because being Ukrainian is a matter of honor.

Glory to Ukraine!

[Author's note: Kateryna still lives with her family in Kyiv. Since then, the Ukrainian national football team and Mstyslav Chernov have all been outfitted by her clothing brand, Indposhiv.]

By Taïsia Klochko

Date of birth: August 25, 1988
From: Kyiv
Profession: Director of Communications at Watu Credits, Kenya
In Kyiv at the start of the invasion; left for Mombasa, Kenya on July 4, 2022.

September 13, 2022

A letter to those who will come after us.

I wasn't afraid of war. On February 23, I had a boxing training session, the next one was scheduled for February 25 at 5:00 pm. When we made an appointment with the trainer for that date, I had the feeling that the training wouldn't take place; I don't know why. Since I've lived in the center of Kyiv since I was a child (I like to jokingly say that I live in the former city of Yaroslav the Wise, because from my windows I can see Saint Sophia of Kyiv), I didn't hear the explosions the next morning. Nobody wrote or called me. When I opened my eyes, I realized that something serious had happened. Messages from people I knew on Facebook: "Explosions are being heard," "Kharkiv is being bombed," and "Soldiers in Kyiv." Then the president's speech. I immediately understood that this was Russia's war against my country. I had no illusions that it was going to end any time soon, but neither did I realize the scale of the invasion.

My mind was made up: I would stay with my parents in Kyiv. I was sure that the city would have to fight, and who would support the men? Who would resist? Who could clear the rubble from the buildings and help the wounded?

I remember the first night. The roar of the planes in the sky. I didn't know if they were ours or those of the enemy. That was the night I realized I could die, perish . . . I don't know what the exact term is. I remember very clearly that I wasn't feeling sorry for myself and that I knew I'd achieved a lot in my life, that I'd had a lot of good times, that I had nothing to regret, that I hadn't put anything off. I went to sleep. The next morning, I got a call from my boss: "What are you doing?" "I was asleep, I just woke up," I told him. His reply: "I'll give you fifteen minutes. Then it's the team meeting. We will think about how we can help the armed forces."

So it was from that call that I started working at the front. What I haven't mentioned yet: before the recent changes in my professional life, I was director of the Fuel and Energy Association of Ukraine. We started supporting our army by supplying fuel.

In those days, there were large reserves of diesel and less petrol. We supplied the land defenses in the Chernihiv, Zhytomyr, Odesa, and Kyiv regions. That's all there was to it.

Fuel. We were lucky, considering the events of the time. At the start of the war, Ukraine had a large quantity of diesel, which was supposed to be used for sowing, but was now almost exclusively destined for military equipment and public utility vehicles. For example, territorial defense used up to three tons of diesel in forty-eight hours. Ironically, the fuel used by the Ukrainian army was imported from Belarus. So our soldiers fought the enemy with their own fuel... But the irony soon came to an end when supplies were almost exhausted after the first month and a half of war, and there were still no alternative supply markets. With every successful delivery, I cried and laughed at the same time. I knew we were going to win.

I don't remember how much fuel we gave, but I do remember the four hundred liters of diesel for Chernihiv. It was late March or early April. Chernihiv had been bombed several times. There was hardly any drinking water or food. People were recharging their cell phones using solar panels. Only one bridge was still intact. A phone call. "We need diesel. We only have four hundred liters left. Bring it here." It turned out that the Kyiv exit roadblock was extended and we couldn't leave. We planned to leave right afterward. At night. The only bridge leading to Chernihiv was destroyed. Despair. How are we going to deliver? "There's still a crossing of the Desna, which dates back to the Second World War." "And how are we going to do it?" "Like our grandfathers, with boats." Four days later. The diesel is in Chernihiv. And for the first time, I saw through the window that flowers were being sold again in the kiosk across the street.

The search for partners to supply diesel and gasoline from the European Union to Ukraine proved adventurous. At first, it was desperate. Nobody wanted to cooperate. Then joy when the first contracts were signed. We learned from potential partners that they themselves had to rigorously calculate fuel reserves for their citizens, and that governments would limit exports of this strategic product. How did this help me if we couldn't meet the growing demand? The European Union was also slow to understand that *business as usual* with Russia or Belarus was no longer an option and that it needed to increase its own production, which would also provide fuel for Ukraine.

A friend called me. "There's a seat on an evacuation train to Warsaw." I said "No. I'm not leaving Kyiv. I'm staying here until the end."

The sirens didn't scare me. On the contrary, they were like a call to resistance. Every time I heard them, I phoned the companies with even more determination to find out what fuel was available. My parents and I never went to the shelter. Somehow, I was convinced that we'd be needed upstairs to help when the houses were destroyed and the victims had to be brought out.

The struggle on the front and the struggle against sleep. Yes, I have to admit, for the first month, I wanted to sleep all the time. I don't know why, but that's how it was. At some point, I disconnected and fell into a very deep sleep that many would probably have envied.

What more can I say about myself? I prayed all the time; sometimes I had no other choice. And I knew I wanted to change the world. I wanted

to become a Ukrainian who changed lives, who protected, and who helped. When I had the opportunity to work in Kenya and help people, I didn't hesitate for a moment.

I've been living in Mombasa for two months now, working for a local company. I'm still helping Ukraine, especially financially, but I'm very happy to have the opportunity to work here in Kenya. After the experience of war, one perceives everything differently, appreciating the smallest things: the sea and the possibility of jogging early in the morning without the wail of sirens, communicating with local people, helping them to realize their dreams and creating businesses, the constantly sunny and warm weather. Of course, I miss my friends scattered all over the world, my family, and my beloved Kyiv. My goal, like that of all Ukrainians, is to change the world for the better, and that's why I'm happy here.

My message to those who come after us is: don't be afraid. Fight. Offer your protection. Don't get distracted. Don't procrastinate. Keep the light within you. And remember, crying has never brought freedom to anyone, fighting is winning the world.

[Author's note: Taïsia returned to Ukraine in 2023, believing that her place was here. She now works at the American Chamber of Commerce with the primary goal of creating favorable legislative and regulatory changes to attract investment to rebuild her country.]

By Oksana Korchynska

Date of birth: November 17, 1970
From: Kyiv
Profession: Member of the Verkhovna Rada (Parliament of Ukraine) from 2014 to 2019 and medical coordinator of the evacuation routes since 2014

November 21, 2022

Today is a quiet day. Only a few wounded have been brought to our stabilization point near the front. But we'll see what happens in the evening.

Paramedics were unable to bring a seriously injured man...

I'll never get used to that. A twenty-four-year-old lieutenant. A perfect face, very handsome. Why do our dead often have such regular, noble features? Now there's a bereavement in another Ukrainian family, it's our common bereavement...

An artillery shell or an S-300 missile explodes somewhere in the distance. It's quiet today, unlike yesterday! In addition to the many wounded soldiers, we regularly save the lives of civilians.

This summer, we worked at a stabilization point in a village close to the front, in a former district hospital. We were bombarded by grenade launchers. In a residential area. It's often bombed. We heard screams. A seriously wounded young civilian is brought to the hospital...

Traumatic amputation of one leg and severe tissue damage to the other. She also suffers from ankylosing spondylitis. This disease makes it difficult to insert a catheter.

The only civilian doctor, Konstantin, and our military medics fought for an hour to save her life. She's a strong woman, her name is Oksana, she's thirty-two, she has a daughter. We evacuated her. On the way, I asked her what she was doing here, as the village had been razed to the ground by the Russians for months. She replied that this was her family's garden and that she had come from near Dnipro to make sure the fruit and vegetables didn't rot. Unfortunately, civilians continue to live in the villages and towns on the front line. They cling to their usual lives. For many, it is more frightening to flee, to throw themselves into the unknown, than to risk death.

Recently, the Russians bombed a village in the hinterland with cluster munitions. A village where there had never been any military personnel. The villagers who survived had to be evacuated by military medics. All the houses have been destroyed. There are corpses in the houses and courtyards. For some reason, the villagers thought they would be safe there. They either didn't think or didn't manage to run to the basement. We're waiting for the wounded.

The first was an elderly woman whose body had been shredded by large bomb fragments. She was no longer breathing, and military medics tried to resuscitate her on the way, but her internal organs were shredded.

Fifteen minutes later, they bring in a slim girl who looks about fifteen. Her name is Anastasiia, and she's nineteen. The military nurse who brought her comes to see me, gives me a piece of paper with her phone number, and asks me to give it to the girl if she needs money or help . . . We bandage her wound and Anastasiia never stops thanking the military nurses who look after her. She thanks them again. I can't help myself and stroke her blond head. "Thank you, Auntie," she says, "but where's my mom? We brought her before me." We all had a lump in our throat when we realized that the dead woman was her mother . . . We didn't dare tell her. Her father has been dead for years, all her neighbors are dead. Now she's all alone. But how are we going to tell her?

There must be a distant relative in Dnipro. We're looking for small clothes, as the volunteers only bring men's sizes for the wounded. We send Anastasiia to a Dnipro hospital for rehabilitation. Our cook Volodymyr comes to offer the help of his wife, who also lives in Dnipro. The next day, she will bring the girl clothes, food, and, above all, a new telephone. Our operating room nurse Natalia also travels to Dnipro. She offers Anastasiia the chance to move to Odesa and live with her family, including her adult daughter, also named Anastasiia . . . Until February 24, 2022, Natalia was a businesswoman, and owner of one of the best veterinary clinics in Odesa, but from the very first days of the attack, she went to the military police station and was mobilized . . .

It may sound trite, but war brings out the worst and the best in people. War has given me an incredible gift: the opportunity to be proud of my people. War always provokes despair, and it strengthens our faith. War constantly brings about miracles . . .

I remember at the very beginning, in 2014, for the protection and intercession of the Virgin Mary, I brought a priest to a tank battalion in Sartana. At the time, I volunteered to help evacuate and treat the wounded in sector M, while also setting up an interdepartmental medical staff to rescue the wounded.

Sartana is a large village near Mariupol, which has been infiltrated by Russian propaganda (and is now completely destroyed by Russian artillery). During the liturgy before communion began, the enemy attacked with heavy artillery. "Keep praying, Father," I told the priest. The bombardment lasted over two hours. Gas pipes exploded, thousands of splinters flew around us and it was impossible to see clearly because of the smoke. The priest gave communion to 116 soldiers during the bombardment. All the soldiers were slightly bruised, including me (I haven't felt a thing since, which sometimes makes life easier in wartime), but nobody was hurt. The Mother of God protected us.

By contrast, thirty meters behind the battalion's fence, horrific things had happened. Dozens of civilians were dead and wounded, body parts hanging in the branches. Many of them had wished that Russia would come to them, and now it had. The death of their loved ones didn't change their minds. We helped them, but in return, they shouted at us: "You fired grenades at us from over there, behind the fence!" It's hard to explain! Moscow's propaganda is stronger than any reality . . .

My comrade Hrek has lived through some miracles. He is one of the best scouts at the front. As he entered the "gray zone," he was hit by a 12.7-caliber bullet. I thought that if a bullet of that caliber hit any part of the body, you wouldn't survive it. He didn't die on the spot. That's the first miracle. The bullet hit the pelvis, spun around, tore off eleven centimeters of the artery, and lodged in the joint. Those who were with him said that blood gushed out over a meter and a half. Almost all the blood came out at once, but he was rescued alive from under the shells. That's the second miracle.

At the Avdiivka stabilization center, he received eight blood bags from eight different people. He was not infected with hepatitis, AIDS, or the Epstein-Barr virus by untested blood donors. This almost never happens. This is the third miracle. Two teams of military doctors managed to stabilize him and transfer him to a hospital in Kharkiv. This is the fourth miracle. He survived eighteen minutes of clinical death, but it had no effect on his memory, his wit, or his humor. He started joking as soon as he regained consciousness. That's the fifth miracle. He didn't die in hospital. That's the sixth miracle. Now he's walking on two legs. That's the seventh miracle. And he's walking along the front line. That's the eighth miracle. Hrek! Watch out for yourself!

In the second month of the great invasion, my comrade Tayra, an excellent and highly experienced first-aider, was captured in Mariupol. The occupiers accused her of being the director of the Azov medical service, of being a Nazi, of harvesting organs from captured Russians and selling them, of taking part in the work of secret American biological laboratories, and so on. She was tortured with electric shocks, beaten, starved and intimidated. Like so many others, she was not to survive the will of her torturers.

Many people in Ukraine have prayed for her. She is a Taekwondo expert and therefore familiar with Eastern ways of thinking. There, in her cell, she wrote the verses Psalm 90 on a cigarette pack with burnt matches and repeated them over and over again.

Soon, people all over the world began to take an interest in her plight. Simple volunteers, frontline nurses, foreign presidents, even Prince Harry. The occupiers decided not to kill her, but to stage a high-profile "trial" in which she would be sentenced to life imprisonment. "A Woman Named Beast" was the title of a program about her broadcast on Moscow television.

And suddenly, just when no one was expecting it, it was switched! Now, it seems like a whim of fate, but when I received the call, I was absolutely certain that I had witnessed a miracle from the Lord! Her first wish after release was to

be baptized. She was baptized by a famous frontline chaplain, Father Serhii, and my husband Dmytro was her godfather . . .

I'm just finishing my report, I haven't managed to get any rest. The volunteer rescuers reported that they were bringing in more wounded.

In the eight months of this large-scale invasion, over six thousand wounded were treated at our stabilization point alone. I try not to count the number of people killed in our region. Every day, we pay a very high price for the freedom of our country. There can be no doubt about our victory. For us, Ukraine and life mean the same thing!

[Author's note: Okasna continues to help and treat the wounded Ukrainians and says it will continue to do so until the war ends.]

By Yuliia Paievska, aka Tayra

Date of birth: December 19, 1968
From: Kyiv
Profession: Paramedic since 2014 and founder of the volunteer medical evacuation and care unit Tayra's Angels
First encounter with war: 2014
In Mariupol at the start of the invasion. After working in a mobile hospital, she was captured by the Russian army on March 16, 2022, before being released on June 17, 2022.

December 16, 2022

After the exchange, I chose my path to recovery: overcoming my health problems through sport.

Meditation and sport have always helped me in the most difficult situations: in civilian life, at the front, and in captivity. So I decided to do things the hard way, in a radical but highly effective way. I'm not in the habit of feeling sorry for myself, because I think all our problems stem from self-pity.

I learned that my place on the team was available and I made up my mind to go to Florida for the competition. It was crazy. There were only three weeks between the time of the exchange and the departure.

At the time of the exchange, I weighed forty-eight kilos. My body was emaciated and I looked like a victim of some kind of concentration camp—the "some kind" being superfluous, since in Russian captivity, you're in a concentration camp . . . By the time I left for training, I weighed fifty kilos. But without training it's very difficult for the body to regenerate. Nevertheless, I did it.

On our return from Florida, we headed to the UK to train with the Ukrainian team before taking part in the *Warrior Games*. We passed through L'viv and decided to visit the Lytchakiv cemetery, as this is where two young men from our team who fell in the ranks of the Ukrainian armed forces during the large-scale Russian invasion are buried.

I was smoking at the grave of Dima Sydoruk, our archery coach. His mother came, and the whole team was there. And I said to myself: My God. Imagine that I'd been torn from life for three months, and in those three months, I'd lost friends. Dima, for example. He was a really great guy, a war hero. I remembered his technical advice and his stories. Dima was seriously wounded during the anti-terrorist operation in eastern Ukraine in 2014. When I looked up, I saw that two rows away was the grave of my friend Sachko Odesa. I didn't know he'd been killed. I froze . . .

I walked over and thought about the time we evacuated a seriously injured man. It was very difficult to keep him alive: the winter, the bitter cold, the numerous wounds, the loss of blood . . . Sashko smiled discreetly from the bottom of his heart, to encourage the wounded man. I did the same, injecting the medicines, checking the tourniquets, and changing the drips. The injured man looked at us and Sachko said: "You'll win. You'll see. Everything's going to be fine."

In the photo at his grave, Sasha looked exactly as he did then: smiling, with the same sincere smile and slightly ironic look. For a second, I thought I heard his voice: "You'll win. You'll see. Everything's going to be great.

There I was, berating myself for having spent three months half-dead in Russian jails instead of saving people. I thought maybe I could have saved Sashko and Dima... Then I turned around and saw the grave of another person I knew. It's impossible to describe the pain.

I've won, as Sashko said. And from now on, everything will be "great." I know it will.

It's very painful for me to go to cemeteries. But I go anyway because I know that heroes die when we forget them.

Rest in peace, little brother.

Later, at the *Warrior Games*, I won two gold medals in swimming, in the fifty- and one hundred-meter freestyle, and a bronze medal in *powerlifting*.

We're going to win!

[Author's note: Despite health problems caused by her imprisonment, Yuliia has returned to the army in the National Brigade "Charter" because she believes she can do more to help Ukraine win. She also writes poetry and a memoir. She exercises and continues to work as a *pro bono* goodwill ambassador for Ukraine, exposing Russian war crimes.]

By Sophia Podkolsina

Date of birth: September 25, 1998
From: Berdyans'k
Profession: History student; wants to become an activist
In Berdyans'k at the start of the invasion; escaped the occupation on March 25, 2022 and now lives in Kyiv.

August 5, 2022

In memory of Roman Ratushnyi and all Ukrainians who fought for our future, in peace and war.

I've always thought of myself as a happy person. I was born into a large family and was surrounded by love and care from an early age. I don't know what the general principle of happiness is, but in my case, it's family and friends. They are my support, my backing, and my inspiration. An inexhaustible source of love and knowledge from which I draw every day, and for which I am infinitely grateful.

Ukraine has always been the leitmotif of my life. When I say "Ukraine," I mean it in the broadest sense, of course. Now that I'm an adult, I consider myself first and foremost a Ukrainian from a social point of view, but in the past, when I was a child, Ukrainian was for me closely linked to my family. Belonging to this nation has always meant protection for me, warm evenings with my family, the gentle Sea of Azov on whose shores I grew up, my mother's smile, and the majestic blue and yellow flag in the city's central square.

The realization of what Ukraine is all about came quite naturally to me.

When I entered the first grade, the Orange Revolution took place. People were protesting because democratic elections had been stolen from them. For Ukrainians, who were finally breathing freedom after seventy years of Soviet occupation and were no longer prepared to tolerate the tyranny of the empire, any manifestation of dictatorship or restriction of their freedom was unacceptable.

The Orange Revolution thus shaped a little first-grader's first ideas about what Ukraine is, what democracy is, and who Ukrainians are. And why we are prepared to fight so hard and with such conviction for our freedom and the right to choose our lives.

I remember New Year's Day 2004/2005 when thousands of people marched through Kyiv's central square to claim what was rightfully theirs. I remember sitting with my aunt in her Kyiv apartment, while my parents and older brother were among the demonstrators on the Maidan. We were watching the live broadcast on an old Soviet television set. And I remember how excited I was to see so many people in the central square, standing in the cold, celebrating the New Year in a new, democratic Ukraine. It's hard to describe in words.

I think a lot of people can't understand what I mean if they haven't experienced something comparable. When you see such a unity of people, something deep awakens in you. A crazy pride, an inner strength, a sincere love for each person who is here now, with you. These feelings were repeated ten years later when I was fifteen and on the Maidan myself during the Revolution of Dignity.

And even if you're a little kid watching the Great Revolution on TV, you realize at that moment that you're part of this society. Of course, you can always distance yourself from it. We're a country of free people, and no one is obliged to identify with this society.

In 2004, I became Ukrainian without knowing it. In 2013/2014, it was a conscious decision.

I didn't realize what had happened in 2004/2005 until later when I became interested in history. It gave me answers to most of the questions I had about my country. It was thanks to my father that I first learned about my country's history. I loved to sit with him in the evenings after dinner and listen to stories about the days of Kyiv Rus', the Soviet dissidents, the conquest of Kyiv by the Muscovite prince Bogolyubsky in 1169, and the beginnings of our democracy. Back then, I was a child and my father was an undisputed authority. It seemed to me that he knew everything. So I recorded every word and retained everything he told me.

Ironically, later, after my history studies, I had many debates with him and refuted some of his theses on historical events. Despite all our historical disputes, we did and still do agree on one thing: Ukraine is an independent democratic state. It has a different culture, language, political system, etc. from Russia.

The Russians' claim that we are "one people," and "one country," irritates me to no end. It's a blatant lie that the Russian empire is spreading all over the world to justify its crimes against humanity. Ukraine and Russia have never been one country. Never have been.

In 1918, the Ukrainians declared their independence. They fought for it for four years, until the Soviet government finally occupied Ukraine for good. I deliberately use the term "occupation," because the Soviet Union is seen by many as a voluntary union of republics. In reality, the Communists used weapons and fear to force other states to submit to them. They were all drenched in the blood of the Communist revolution and forcibly integrated into the greatest totalitarian system in human history.

I can't help thinking of the sacrifices made back then by the fighters for Ukraine to be able to live in their own free country. Today, it's somehow much easier for Ukraine. Although it is fighting against an empire, it enjoys the undisputed support of the world, our voice is heard, and our right to exist is not questioned. A hundred years ago, we were alone. And this struggle demanded enormous strength and courage.

This part of my letter concerns me indirectly. But the second part of this historical digression concerns me directly. My studies have enabled me to link the history of the world to the history of my family.

My great-grandmother Marfa was born between 1914 and 1919 in a small village in the Poltava region. She always said she'd forgotten when she was born and never celebrated her birthday. This may be true, but I suspect that my great-grandmother simply didn't want to reveal her age, and enjoyed having everyone wonder how old she really was.

Marfa was born at a time of great upheaval. Her life was therefore a difficult one. While still a child, she lost both her parents. Her mother died at birth, and her father soon afterward of typhus or Spanish flu. Marfa and her two sisters were raised by their grandfather, but he too soon died.

My great-great-great-grandfather Deviatchenko was a weaver and prosperous peasant. However, in 1930, the Soviet government announced its policy of "dekulakization." Simply put, the peasants were violently dispossessed of their property. Marfa's grandfather was dispossessed of everything: the land he owned, his cattle, his horses, his labor. Everything went to the kolkhoz, to the state.

I can't imagine what it's like for a man to have his life's work, into which he had poured his soul and which he wanted to pass on to his descendants, taken away from him. Yet, "thanks" to Russia, my family had a similar experience almost a hundred years later, but let's put things in order.

Deviatchenko couldn't bear the blow and died shortly afterward, leaving the three girls orphans. A few years later, Ukraine was hit by the Great Famine, organized by the Soviets. The Holodomor claimed the lives of millions of Ukrainians and instilled fear and obedience in them for generations to come. I saw this for myself when I listened to the stories of my great-grandmother who, even seventy years later, was still afraid to talk about that period. After all, you never know when Russia will come to take your bread. Here again, a link with the present comes to mind, and I have to mention the theft of Ukrainian grain from the occupied territories. Russian blackmail of hunger. The methods have not changed.

Marfa and her sisters survived because they walked to Donets'k in 1932/1933 to work in a Soviet factory. Simply because the workers were fed at the factory. I can't even begin to imagine what it's like to walk more than three hundred kilometers to find something to eat. Because there's literally nothing to eat at home.

It was in Donets'k that Marfa met her future husband, my great-grandfather Vassyl Podkolsin. He came from the Kursk region, where many Ukrainians lived until the 1930s. He too was fleeing famine . . .

My grandfather Volodymyr Vassyliovytch was born in 1939. That year, two totalitarian regimes signed a mutual agreement and began the bloodiest war in history. A war that twice swept across Ukrainian territory.

Two years later, my great-grandfather was sent to the front and Marfa was left alone with two young children. In his last letter to her, Vassyl wrote: "I have gone to defend your Ukraine..."

Shortly afterward, Marfa learned that he had disappeared. For the rest of her life, she would wait for her husband to return. Every time she saw an outsider enter the courtyard, she would rush to the door in the hope of catching a glimpse of her beloved's face. In her home, the wedding photo still hangs on the wall next to the icon.

My great-grandmother Marfa later returned to her native village, where my grandfather Volodymyr grew up. Those who knew him during his lifetime described him as a cheerful man. My mother once said of her stepfather: "If he were alive today, he would be a millionaire. In the Soviet Union, of course, it was impossible to become a millionaire (legally). Everyone had to be equally poor."

My grandfather's character did not allow him to become a mediocre factory worker. The realities of the socialist country demanded that people either live on the edge of poverty and scarcity or bend the law to support themselves and their families. Given my grandfather's temperament, the second option was obvious to him. He saw the shortcomings of the Soviet system and, like most of the country's citizens at the time, looked for ways to circumvent the law.

I can't find the right words to describe him. He was a born businessman but had the misfortune to be born in a country where private property could not exist. Everything had to belong to the state. He should have been born in twentieth-century America. In a country where hard-working, dedicated people are respected. He was born in a country where no one was allowed to earn money on their own.

Under Brezhnev, the underground economy and black market flourished in the USSR. People engaged in black trade (resale of rare goods), did business underground, and so on. It's interesting to note that the official authorities were aware of these activities, but didn't look at them too closely. In historiography, this is known as the "limit of permissible resistance." In most cases, when a regime is going through an existential crisis, it allows people to circumvent the law to prevent protests. However, it is also necessary to maintain the illusion that the state is acting against illegal activities. That's why the most unfortunate ended up in Soviet prisons.

Volodymyr Vassyliovytch was imprisoned twice by the Soviets for his clandestine affairs. Prison hadn't changed him, he remained the same kind, smiling person he used to be, but I'll never forgive the Soviet regime for taking a part of my grandfather's life simply because he wanted to earn his own money. His wife, my grandmother Lidia, had to raise her children alone at the age of thirty. My

father, a seventeen-year-old cadet, had to look after his sick mother and younger sister because his father was in prison.

As my father recounted, my grandfather sometimes lost his temper and, in a fit of anger, spoke of a free Ukraine. I still know very little about this part of his life, but I have reason to believe that he met Ukrainian dissidents, who were then being held en masse in Soviet prisons. And perhaps he became one of them himself.

The conclusion of all this is quite simple: Russia has brought nothing good to my country, my family, and me. Although, no, it would be more accurate to put it this way: Russia has brought nothing but suffering and pain to my country, my family, and myself.

When I was fifteen, when the criminal pro-Russian president Victor Yanukovych was following Russia's instructions and thought he had the right to determine how Ukrainians should vote, the revolt of dignity began in the country.

In the autumn of 2013, my father went to the Maidan and joined the protesters. Back then, at the start of these events, I again followed the revolution on TV. Now I was aware of what was happening. I didn't need anyone to explain to me why Ukrainians were protesting. Why Russia is not our friend and never has been. I didn't need anyone to explain to me the enormous threat this empire posed to Ukraine's existence.

Back then, the mood of the people in Berdyans'k, where I grew up, was different. Generally speaking, you could say that this is a pro-Russian region, where nostalgic memories of the Soviet Union still predominate.

I'm in no way denying people the right to self-determination, and I can't forbid anyone to identify with the Russian people. However, when Russian rhetoric speaks of "protecting Russians in Ukraine," it's a lie. Their "protection," both in the past and today, consists of destroying everything Ukrainian. In his speech on February 24, 2022, Putin defended the thesis that Ukraine did not exist as a country and that there should therefore be no Ukrainians. This is how the representative of a people erased my existence.

If I don't forbid Russians to call themselves Russian, why do they forbid me to call myself Ukrainian? Why wasn't it so easy to speak Ukrainian in regions where Russian propaganda was influential? Why couldn't I place orders in Ukrainian in the Ukrainian town of Berdyans'k? Can you imagine a Spaniard not being able to order coffee in Spanish in Valencia?

It's not for nothing that most Ukrainians in the eastern regions became aware of the danger of Russian myths with the outbreak of full-scale war in 2022. It's hard to understand why a country that claims to be your friend would suddenly fire an artillery shell at your house.

But I'm jumping ahead. It's still 2013, Ukraine is in the throes of a revolution, and the eastern regions of Ukraine are mostly listening to Russian propaganda.

Ukrainians' lack of knowledge of their own history was particularly evident at this time. In the context of the Revolution of Dignity, towns like Berdyans'k organized so-called anti-Maidan demonstrations alongside pro-Ukrainian rallies. I remember people I knew well losing their credibility in my eyes. I remember school teachers suddenly talking about the "small culture of Ukraine" and the "great Russian people." I remember how, in class, they wished death on those who took to the streets in Kyiv and other cities to protest against the criminal government and defend their right to democratic elections. I remember heated exchanges in which people spoke to me in Russian propaganda phrases. And I remember the horror this caused me.

They saw not just Ukraine, but the whole world through this prism. The West was the enemy, NATO a criminal alliance bent on Russia's destruction, and Ukraine an uncontrolled state in need of "strong leadership like Putin." From this perspective, Russia was naturally presented as Ukraine's "big brother" and "savior."

But I was also lucky enough to meet people for whom Ukraine's European course was obvious. Obvious, because Ukraine is naturally part of Europe from a historical point of view. It's only because of Russian propaganda that much of the world thinks otherwise. With Europe, we share common values, we respect the rule of law and when it is violated, we protest.

At the beginning of winter, I also went to Kyiv. And once again I felt the unity I remembered from my childhood. I saw young students cooking for others. I saw businessmen in luxury cars bringing various items and food for the demonstrators. I saw people organizing the construction of barricades. All in all, I saw enthusiastic, smiling people everywhere, who believed in a promising future for their country.

On February 18, 2014, the first shots were fired. I was at home at the time, my father was in Kyiv at the epicenter of the events. It was the first time Ukrainians had suffered such a painful loss. I can't find the words to describe the sadness, the pain, and the shock. The people who died then were called the Heavenly Centuries. They were the first to give their lives for a free Ukraine in this bloody war that continues to this day.

For me, it had been obvious since 2014 that Russia was going to attack Ukraine again. Like most people, I naturally hoped for a peaceful solution to the conflict, but common sense and logic always told me that this was virtually impossible. Russia is an empire, and every empire either expands or collapses.

Perhaps you were hoping to read more in my letter about what happened to me after February 24, 2022. However, I can't say anything about that without explaining my background. I hope you'll forgive me.

On February 24, I was in my hometown of Berdyans'k. I felt the need to go home because of all the reports of an impending war.

In the month before the attack, I tried to convince my family to draw up an emergency plan. But my family was in the same state as most Ukrainians. They simply didn't want to believe it. They hoped that Russia would soon withdraw its troops, because who would have the idea of attacking so openly?

Russia had the idea. And it attacked openly and illegally. Above all, it is an act of undisguised humiliation of the countries of Europe and America. Typical behavior for a terrorist state.

Before the war, I had panic attacks. I couldn't sleep, I couldn't think about anything except the catastrophe that was coming our way. So I decided to go home. My train arrived in Berdyans'k on the evening of February 23. That evening, the president declared martial law, and we sat around the table, watching the news and even cracking jokes. My father wanted to go to the military police station because he's a reservist, and I made a list of things I wanted to do the next day.

On February 24, I was awakened at 5:30 a.m. by a call from my older brother.

"Hello, why can't I reach any of you?!"

"What's happened? Did someone die for you to call so early?"

"Wake up, it's started . . ."

As I write these words, I begin to tremble as I did then. I think I'll remember for the rest of my life those first hours when I learned that a full-scale war had begun. The confusion and fear were there.

We packed up and prepared to leave. No one knew the extent of the situation, no one knew how far the occupiers had advanced. My father and younger brother went to reconnoiter and returned an hour later.

"That's it, they're already in the town. We have no territorial defense, the Ukrainian troops have withdrawn, and there's no one to defend the city."

At our peril, we left the city to join our friends in the village. I spent three days there. To be honest, I slept most of the time. It was like being in a trance. And when I woke up, I was watching the news and couldn't make any sense of it. Although I'd been preparing for this war for eight years, my body refused to accept what was happening.

But then a miracle happened. Ukraine resolutely repelled the first Russian attacks, despite considerable losses. I call that a miracle because when something happens that nobody believes in, it's a miracle.

It's hard to explain how much strength it gave us. I've seen videos of captured occupiers who didn't expect such resistance, and destroyed Russian equipment, and videos of our soldiers encouraging us not to lose heart.

"If there is a God, he wears the uniform of the Ukrainian armed forces." It's impossible to measure what Ukrainian soldiers achieved in the first days of the war. It's not just about military success. It's about the way they saved the whole country from mass panic and convinced us that we were going to win no matter what. And they prove it every day.

My father went to war on February 26. And I returned to Berdyans'k with my family. Today it seems a disastrous decision, but at the time we were convinced that our army would quickly drive the Russians out of the country. So it was better to wait at home. This decision turned into the occupation.

On February 27, the Russians took the city. And for me, another miracle happened. The inhabitants, whom I had always considered pro-Russian, took to the streets, unarmed and carrying Ukrainian flags, and began singing the Ukrainian anthem in front of the Russian military. For them, Russia no longer existed as an ally and friend. For some long ago, for others since the last three days of the war. They shouted at the Russians to leave Ukraine, and the occupiers looked at them quizzically, not understanding why they weren't happy to see them.

The protests lasted a month. Over time, the Russians realized that they would not find support here and began to use their usual methods: kidnapping, intimidation, and violence. Despite this, the protests continued until most people had left the city for the area controlled by the Ukrainian government.

This month, I followed the news constantly. I was always waiting for reports of a counter-attack. And I prayed that the Russians wouldn't get to my family first. I trembled at every rustle in the yard, I was afraid to go downtown and I even had a knife on me. To reassure myself. I had no time to prepare, because what could I do against an armed Russian soldier?

In town, there was less and less food. I remember that in the early days of the war, people bought everything, and no new goods were delivered. The first things to run out were medicines. Then basic food. Russian reality was getting closer and closer.

When the first reports of kidnappings of public figures appeared, I insisted that we leave. My father is a well-known Ukrainian activist in Berdyans'k. So it was only a matter of time before the Russians came to us.

The Ukrainian government was negotiating green corridors with the Russians, which we also wanted to use. But it was a trap, of course. Normally, the journey from Berdyans'k to Zaporizhzhia—where the inhabitants of Berdyans'k used to go—takes two hours. We traveled for two days.

When the Ukrainian authorities set up a corridor for the civilian population, the Russians deliberately installed checkpoints at every junction. A convoy of around one thousand vehicles had to stop every ten kilometers to be checked. The men were particularly frisked, and some were not allowed to continue on their way. My younger brother, who was fifteen at the time, had to undress several times and be checked for "nationalist tattoos." The closer we got to government-controlled territory, the more brutal they became.

On the second day of the trip, we hid our cell phones. I had already deleted all the photos and files the Russians didn't want to see. Even if my phone was "clean," the Russians could have taken it from me or broken it. They justified their decision by the fact that the Ukrainians could film the movements of Russian military vehicles, but I think it was just an extra humiliation that they particularly enjoyed.

Late in the evening of the second day, we entered the government-controlled zone. When I saw our flag at the checkpoint, I burst into tears. I was overwhelmed with love for this country and felt like I was breathing for the first time since February 24. I'll never forget that feeling. I understood that I wouldn't let anyone take my country away from me, that I wouldn't let anyone take it from me, and that I would fight for it, to my last breath if need be. That's probably the kind of relief a person feels when they learn they've been cured of cancer. It's the kind of joy a child feels when he hugs his mother, whom he hasn't seen for a long time.

I then moved to a foreign city for a few months, as it was still too dangerous to return to Kyiv. In Berdyans'k, there were no missile attacks, no sirens, and life seemed calmer, but I didn't feel at home. Here, on government-controlled Ukrainian territory, freedom reigned. And it was home, no matter what town I was in.

Everything we had built in our lives we left behind in the occupied city. It's not without reason that I mentioned my ancestor Deviatchenko earlier. In 1930, the Soviets had taken everything from him. In 2022, a few days after leaving Berdyans'k, we learned that the Russians had entered our house and my brother and father's business. Almost a hundred years later, the Russians again took everything they could from my family.

The occupiers questioned anyone who might have information about us. They told one of our acquaintances that the Podkolzins were "enemies of the Russian people." Now these acquaintances, who have recently left the city, have told us about lists of names of people whom the Russians have forbidden to leave the country and have ordered to be captured. Our names are also on these lists. I was lucky enough to leave the city a few days before the persecution began.

Now I'm home, my family is relatively safe and we continue to work with all our might for Ukraine's victory. Just as in 2014 it was my conscious decision to join the Revolution of Dignity, in 2022 it was my conscious decision to stay here. I feel I'm needed here, and above all, despite the missiles, the sirens, despite the war and the war-related restrictions, I feel good here and I belong here.

I know how difficult it is for those who have escaped the war and gone abroad. Every day, I read testimonies of how much they miss their country and how much they want to return. And I am infinitely grateful and proud that Ukrainians, even those who are now abroad, continue to support Ukraine in every way they can, even though they are suffering the stress of war. They go to demonstrations, don't let the world forget about us, and help those who have stayed here. The unity I felt at certain times during our revolutions, I now feel all the time.

So what is Ukraine to me? Probably the same as Germany for Germans, Belgium for Belgians, and Finland for Finns. It's not just laws and state institutions. It's your parents' home, coffee in your favorite café, discussions with friends, a walk in the park. It's the metro in Kyiv, fresh bread in the morning at the grocery store, rush-hour traffic jams, and my beloved Sea of Azov. For the first time in my life, I won't be swimming there this summer because of the Russians...

But above all, of course, it's the people. Ukraine is its people. They are rising from the ashes, finding the strength to fight and keep working despite all the horrors the terrorist empire has inflicted on our country. For themselves and for their children's future.

I always thought I was a happy person. And strangely enough, it was the war that convinced me that I was really happy to have been born among such incredible people.

[Author's note: Married in April 2025, she still lives in Kyiv, where she works as head of analytics at a media monitoring company.]

By Meriam Yol

Date of birth: April 3, 1994
From: Kharkiv
Profession: Producer
In Kharkiv at the start of the invasion

September 24, 2022

I had intended to start this letter in chronological order, i.e. on February 24, 2022, but I'll probably have to start a little earlier.

It was an evening in October 2016, I think. I was sitting in a bar with a friend I was working with at the time. A good acquaintance from Russia had come to visit. We were working at a communications school at the time and often invited teachers from Russia to give classes. The Russian guest was very talented, interesting, and had incredible professional experience. What's more, he was a very nice person. We were very enthusiastic about him.

Then I went out for a cigarette. Apparently, you could tell the evening had gone really well. So much so that an acquaintance I found smoking asked me why I was so happy. And I replied: "A friend from Moscow is here and we're having a perfect evening." Her face changed. She asked me in a rather sharp tone how I could sit at the same table with someone from Russia. At the time, I didn't understand her radicalism. Not at the time.

Want to read about Ukrainian feelings? Here's the first: *guilt*.

Yes, Russia started the war in my country long before February 24, 2022; it all started long before that, in 2014. I was twenty then. I remember the Maidan and the Revolution of Dignity. I went to the rallies in Kharkiv, I cried when I arrived in Kyiv on the avenue of the Heavenly Centuria. I remember Crimea, Donets'k, and Luhansk. But that was all. It was somehow forgotten, erased, and covered by many other things and preoccupations. And many of us Ukrainians unfortunately didn't pay it the attention it deserved. The events that began in February opened the eyes of many of us.

On February 24, I woke up alone in my bed at 5:00 a.m. My husband was sitting in the kitchen, he hadn't slept all night because he had a premonition: it was going to start at any moment. In the last month before the invasion, I was preparing a big joint project with European partners, and in the last week, when all the international media were already talking about the possible invasion, I wrote national press releases to say that our project had to go ahead anyway. Because "as long as we can do something, we will."

I didn't think this could happen to me in the twenty-first century, in my own country. How wrong I was.

The only thing my husband had managed to convince me to do a few days before the war was to pack an emergency backpack, just in case. But we had no intention of leaving.

The negation.

The first feeling I had. The feeling: this isn't possible.

I later learned that the five phases of acceptance (denial, anger, bargaining, depression, and acceptance) can be experienced in a circle. I've been going through these phases for almost seven months, like on a rollercoaster.

At 5:05 a.m., we hear explosions, we try to get information, all chats are interrupted, and the question "How are you?" appears every second on the screens of all our friends at home and abroad. We're sitting on the floor in the hallway, we don't yet know anything about the "two-wall rule," but we intuitively do the right thing.

At 5:50 a.m., my mother sends me a photo from the window of her and my grandmother's house: a military base is on fire. They live on the outskirts of the city, in northern Saltivka.

At 6:00 a.m., we get a call from our friends; they're leaving town and ask us if we'd like to come with them, they still have room in the car. We say no. They ask us if they should let us have the keys to their café and bakery, where they have their own well-equipped cellar. We think for a few seconds and say yes.

And then, the first three weeks are almost like a day: we stay in the café basement and welcome people, cats, dogs, chinchillas, rabbits, and fish.

Since February 25, we've been baking bread (in our friends' bakery, as their food supplies and capacities allow) and helping our neighbors.

Our boys register as volunteers with the Kharkiv regional administration.

Along with many others, we send photos and reports of events to the international media, some of us walking fearlessly around the city and photographing the effects of the first rocket and artillery fire. We give many interviews. We try to reach a wide audience. Alongside humanitarian aid.

We barely sleep. We read the news non-stop. We hear the first sirens and impacts, rifle bursts outside the window. We still believe that people in Russia will go to demonstrations, so we try to reach them.

The most frightening sound I've ever heard in my life was the whistle of fighter jets over downtown Kharkiv in early March.

The most beautiful flowers were the ones the boys found for us on March 8: tulips, five bouquets of tulips. Can you imagine?

We had a wife at home who was eight months pregnant and we googled how to deliver a baby. Our friend was in the Kharkiv regional administration on March 1 and miraculously survived only because he ran quickly downstairs after the first impact. A second missile landed where he had been sleeping, passing through all the floors down to the basement.

Then there was *hatred*. And it was the engine, the fuel for all our activities over the next three months. Every time I read about people killed, children raped, houses destroyed, torture, and terrorist attacks, every time I saw with my own eyes the destruction of my city, I was angry, and that gave me strength.

In mid-March, we started volunteering on a grand scale. The staff of the agency I'd worked for the last eight years left the city almost in their entirety on the first day. While we were active in Kharkiv, they very quickly opened a donation fund in Transcarpathia, under more or less calm circumstances, and set up a website, call center, and customer relationship management system to receive orders from Kharkiv residents for food, medicines, hygiene products, first-aid items for children and animals, as well as evacuation requests.

My husband and I continued to sleep in the cellar, but we started going to the hub every day. My field was pharmaceuticals. It's funny, my grandparents are doctors and they always wanted me to follow the same path. I chose a different path, but medicine caught up with me anyway.

It was very difficult. We received truckloads of humanitarian aid from various countries. I tried to cope with the countless boxes of medicines, whose packaging and leaflets contained explanations in Italian, Georgian, Turkish, Spanish, and Hebrew. I tried to understand the active ingredients, properties, and dosages.

The days were very similar, the requests and orders were pouring in, we gave ourselves our first day off on May 8, and I think we only did this because there were reports of possible mass provocations by the Russians and we didn't want to endanger our volunteer drivers.

We returned to our apartment on day 109, in June. And for the first time after four months in Kharkiv, we left the city for two days to go to L'viv.

When I came back from there, I was infinitely sad. During all the time we had lived in Kharkiv in a state of war, first we got used to the fear, then we were no longer afraid. We got used to the explosions. To the empty streets, to the green military vehicles, to the impenetrable darkness of the evening, to the stars in the sky, which had never been as visible in the big city as they were in the mountains. We didn't get used to the idea that there was "no life" in my town. Because there had been, and there still is. We'd go to concerts in a secret place in the cellar, watch films about the Slovo house, and see a theatrical performance ourselves. My friends even got married in Kharkiv in the summer. After L'viv, however, I was sad. Not because there was life in L'viv, no, no, but because Russia had deprived my city Kharkiv of such a normal life.

The last two months of summer were followed by *depression*. We continued our volunteer work, but the hardest part, I think, was continuing to do it all. Every day. Every day the same thing. The same daily routine. Like a never-ending day. And then, up until February 24, we'd all been doing very different things, less "on the line."

And all around us, many people are coming back and many people are leaving. Some are returning because they can no longer live without their homes. Others are leaving because it's hard to live in a town close to the front line. It's hard to work, it's hard emotionally because our damn neighbor is playing Russian roulette with us every night, dropping S-300s and Iskanders on our town.

And then our army performed a miracle and liberated a large part of the Kharkiv region in early September. And now we have a new wave of emotions. We have gone from hatred to thirst for life. From voluntary help to faith. Dreams amidst death. Our daily routine: requests for help from the big foundations, receiving universal first-aid kits, because people have been under occupation for six months and haven't seen any medicine at all. Receiving an incredible number of food and hygiene packs. Non-stop work. Fatigue. Inspiration. And faith again.

What is happening to us, to our city, to our country, is incredible. It's both terrible and incredible. If someone had told me that I would see even 10% of this with my own eyes, I would have called them an idiot. I never thought I'd understand my great-grandmother, who stocked up on food and other things after the Second World War. And now I have a bag of gas masks in the hallway. Just in case. I never thought that a sentence from our messages such as "You can't cook, only the kettle works," would leave me stunned. Never in my life did I think I'd hear on the phone: "Thank you for the medication, my wife has passed away, we'll pass it on, but thank you so much for your help." I never thought my friends would fight. I never thought I'd be so happy when strangers were released from captivity. I would never have thought that "two hundred" was a matter of death and not a coffee bill. I would never have thought that the first thing that would come to mind right after the word "kind" would be "artillery fire." I would never have imagined that at dinner with friends, we would remain silent for a long time after learning of another person's death.

What our people are doing now, how they are uniting and helping each other, is just incredible. All the fund-raising for military needs, the help with housing for displaced persons, the cars donated for the front, and the volunteers. All the teas and sandwiches were served in railway stations. All the little and big things.

The fact that we, Ukraine and Russia, are truly different peoples with different values has become obvious to the whole world, and above all to ourselves. As the saying goes: "If Russia stops fighting, there will be no more war; if Ukraine stops fighting, there will be no more Ukraine."

We know there's still a lot of work to be done. Both now, during the war, and after our victory. But the most important thing is that we are clear about why we are doing this, and what a terrible price we are paying for our freedom. So my final sentiment is *faith*: in our armed forces, in our volunteers, in our economy, in our people, in our best country in the world.

[Author's note: Meriam works as the Chief Operating Officer of the NGO Volonteerska. She is still in Kharkiv, helping the defence forces and civilians, and working on the reconstruction of the city's destroyed cultural heritage.]

By Dina Vong

Date of birth: June 13, 1993
From: Chernihiv
Profession: TV presenter, journalist
First encounter with war: Odesa in 2014
In Chernihiv at the start of the invasion

September 9, 2022

Each new day can be my last. I accept it without emotion, with composure and sobriety. I feel no fear, sadness, panic, or other feelings. It's simply a fact. Just like the fact that the wheat is yellow, the sky is blue, there's a war at home, and Russia is a terrorist state. I'm not saying this to elicit sympathy. It's just that this feeling has become a daily thing for me, even though it's essential. I'm trying to do something important because I know there won't be a second chance.

My name is Dina Vonh. I was born in a small town in the Chernihiv region and have been living in Chernihiv for seven years. I'm a journalist and TV presenter. My story and my experiences are probably not unique or significant, but I want to share them. Because tomorrow, a week from now, or a month from now, I could die under the bullets of a Russian missile.

***

I'm writing this text in Russian. Because it's precisely the language that is cited as one of the reasons for this senseless war unleashed by the Russian Federation. In Ukraine, there are quite a few Russian speakers. At least in our region. I explain this by the fact that we have borders with Belarus and Russia. But no one has ever forbidden anyone to speak Russian. No one has. There have been false claims about this, and unfortunately, there still are.

In Ukraine, the official language is Ukrainian. This is perfectly normal. It makes sense for civil servants to speak Ukrainian in public and at work. In their private lives, they can do what they like, but Ukrainian should be spoken during working hours. However, pro-Russian political forces in my country have repeatedly distorted the news. For example, the news that the only official language in Ukraine is Ukrainian has often been interpreted as a principled ban on Russian.

Ironically, language-related attacks tended to be directed at those who spoke Ukrainian. I realized this when I studied in Odesa. My Ukrainian-speaking friends could be insulted on public transport or in a store. People would make fun of them. Even my teachers, who were originally from Odesa, suffered discrimination because they spoke Ukrainian in everyday life.

Many people in Ukraine are now switching to Ukrainian in their daily lives. Not everyone succeeds, and some make a lot of mistakes or use Russianisms. But that's no problem. The most important thing is that we have followed this path. Yes, not everything is ideal, but we are returning to our true roots and freeing ourselves from the influence of Russian propaganda, which harassed us during the thirty-one years of our independence. And we're getting rid of the layers of Soviet propaganda dust with which they tried to wrap our parents. Now we joke, albeit bitterly, that nobody has done as much to popularize our mother tongue as Russia. Russian is now the language of the aggressor in my country, and although many people still use it out of habit, we're changing that and changing little by little.

I'm writing this text in Russian just to show that I can do it, that nobody forbids me to do it, and that I'm not persecuted or hated for it. In my daily life, I speak fluent Ukrainian and Russian. But at work, on social media, and in conversations with friends, my language is Ukrainian. And I'm proud of that. Ukrainian is the language of freedom. Ukrainian is the language of heroes.

Since the start of the full-scale invasion, I've only written one post in Russian on a social network. It was blocked by Facebook because it supposedly incited hatred. Yet all I said was that the Russians were killing us, destroying our cities, and torturing our people. I simply described the facts. From that moment on, I understood that it was impossible to reach the Russians. No matter what language you speak.

***

On February 24, I had Covid. It was the fifth day of my illness, I was weak, and I slept a lot and deeply. No wonder I didn't hear the air raid sirens and explosions. A friend woke me up and said: "The war has started here." I had long understood that war was coming to our home. Since 2014, many people have known that what other countries called the conflict in eastern Ukraine was war in its purest form.

And it was only a matter of time before it spread further. In 2022, the media began reporting on a possible imminent invasion. In February, the number and urgency of these reports increased again. It was obvious that we had been warned. But no one expected it to get this bad. Because you only understand what war means when you come face-to-face with it.

War is the constant sound of artillery fire; it's the noise of planes flying overhead, which frightens many people to the point of cardiac arrest; it's suicides out of fear; it's death from lack of medical care because doctors simply couldn't come because of the shooting and hospitals were destroyed by the enemy; it's death by grenade, bomb or bullet. War is hunger because there was practically nothing to buy in the stores; it is constant thirst and dirt on one's own body, because the Russians had damaged the water supply in Chernihiv, so people had to think hard about what was more important: taking a sip and quenching one's thirst or washing one's hands. War means abandoned and frightened animals. Hungry and miserable. War is the smell of decomposing corpses because mortuaries had no electricity and it wasn't always possible to bury people. What's more, the Russians even bombed the cemetery, which is why Chernihiv residents were also buried in the forest park. And many people were unable to say a proper farewell to their loved ones. War means constant fear for loved ones, to the point where you almost go mad when they don't answer the phone or messages.

We didn't understand all this until later. On the morning of February 24, I packed my emergency bag. I'd already packed the essentials because I knew this would happen sooner or later. I wrote to my employer to offer all the help I could. After all, I had to get healthy anyway, the doctor had said I was no longer contagious, so I was ready to go to the office, even on foot. But the station management had decided to send everyone home so as not to endanger the employees. Our boss and the chief cameraman filmed the whole thing together. They were even the first to document the greatest destruction after the bombing. The others helped out online. We did what we could for as long as we could because that's when the Internet went down.

The cellar of our house had several zones. It was impossible to stay in one of them (where the sewage pipes ran). It was very damp and cold. A second, opposite, was warmer, but that's where most people had gathered. So my neighbors and I stayed in the central area. It was cold and draughty, but at least it was a shelter. And we had a chance of survival.

Of course, there was nothing in our cellar except some rubble and a few "shacks" that some neighbors had put up for them. There weren't even any lights. So the men started laying cables, screwing in light bulbs, and installing benches. Everyone brought what they had—tools for some, extension cords, bottles of water, or canned goods for others. The women brought blankets and insulating mats.

That's when we all finally met. Have you ever noticed that you don't talk much to your neighbors? A standard polite greeting, an exchange of a few polite phrases, and that's it? At home, that's how it was. But then, in the cellar, we learned more about each other. We talked about what was going on outside and reassured each other. And despite the adverse circumstances, it was wonderful. You realize you're living in the same house as some wonderful people.

I'd like to tell you about my neighbor Viktor. He lives on the first floor and has a wife and a teenage daughter. He's the one who organized the men's work. He's the one who built the benches for people to sit on. It was on his initiative that the neighbors began to set up dormitories for the children in the "barracks." They were opened for this purpose. It was warmer in the "barracks," and by installing simple furniture and covering the walls with chipboard, we all together created

at least minimal comfort for our little neighbors. As much as possible. Viktor was the one everyone listened to. And it was thanks to him that everything was in order at home.

I was always reading and listening to the news. Back then, not everyone knew which TV channel to turn on or which radio program to listen to. People were looking for information on Telegram or Viber channels, but there were so many fakes and manipulated messages, so many things that only increased fear and panic. I knew very well which sources were reliable and which were not. Over the seven years, I worked as a journalist, my judgment was honed in this respect. I passed on what I had read on the websites of the army, the head of the military administration, and the city council. And I explained what messages we could look at, what was actually verified and was reliable. So I fulfilled my mission, albeit indirectly.

I fought particularly hard against *fake news*. "The Russians have already entered the city, fighting is taking place on Rokossovsky Street (a street in Chernihiv now renamed Levko-Loukianenko Prospekt)," "Chernihiv has surrendered." These were the most striking messages of those days. And I've convinced people not to believe them. Because in 100% of cases, they had received this information from people who "knew exactly" or who were "military acquaintances." But in reality, it was false information. How was I to know that the information was false? To be honest, I trusted my instincts. Yes, I'm still sure today that the Russians will never take Chernihiv. But at the time, I backed up and confirmed this intuition with evidence from official sources and the contacts I'd made over the years.

We didn't stay in the cellar the whole time. Of course, some people went down the first day and didn't come out of the cellar until they had left the city or the active phase of the fighting was over. I, on the other hand, returned to my sixth-floor apartment immediately after the alert was lifted. I had set up a little rest area in the hallway, where the "two-wall rule" was respected. Of course, this wouldn't have protected me from a bomb dropped by the Air Force.

The first night, I didn't sleep. I lay on the floor, fully dressed in my shoes, and watched the *United News TV Marathon*. It was a project of the major national channels. They had banded together to broadcast news about the situation in the country. The regional channels then picked up these reports. Ours did too. I don't think it's my place to criticize my colleagues or this transmission. But that night of February 25, I didn't understand what was going on. The Kyiv presenter expressed her feelings, and her hatred of the attacker, and the show ended up becoming a spectacle. It really affected me at the time. I had the impression that what was going on wasn't being taken seriously, as if it were all being staged.

I found myself on the floor in the hallway, dressed completely silly, clutching my emergency bag, and I simply misinterpreted the situation. As it turned out, the capital—and probably the whole of Ukraine—didn't understand what was happening in Chernihiv.

***

On the second day, the firing intensified. The noise of the fighting even allowed many people to distinguish enemy fire from our army's return fire. Many people's hearts stopped at every shot. People were afraid for themselves and their loved ones. The second day was not much different from the first. We rushed from the apartment to the cellar. Then from the cellar to the apartment. To cook, to warm up, to wash.

Every day, as long as we had food, we would prepare lunch and take it to the checkpoints where soldiers from other towns stood guard. In this way, we gave them at least one hot meal. Of course, it wasn't much, but we did what we could. It was our contribution. We also collected clothes, socks, and hygiene items. We gave what we still had at home and also tried to buy something. But by the second day (and the first in some areas), the store shelves were almost empty. There was no more cash in the vending machines. At petrol stations, too, there were queues. It was the beginning of the crisis.

Several times, I came home with five loaves of bread from the store. I'd take them to elderly people who couldn't leave the house on their own. I kept one for myself. My neighbors and I would usually try to buy larger quantities, and then share what we got, as we never knew if the shopping trip would be successful. Once, I was able to buy milk. I don't drink it myself, but I knew a neighbor had two young children and needed milk. When I saw the last carton of milk, I didn't think long about it, I took it straight away. Viktor had once managed to buy some sausages and shared them with me. The woman in the next apartment, Iryna, immediately gave me her canned goods and a small supply of potatoes. She worked at the hospital and told me she would be staying there. She took some of her food and left me some. For me or for the neighbors.

I once managed to get into a large supermarket downtown. I had gone with a neighbor. Half an hour after we got home, the Russians dropped bombs on a residential area in the center, on the houses on Chornovil Street. Thirty minutes earlier, we could have been killed or injured by the shock wave.

The bombing of the residential buildings on Chornovil Street took place on March 3. For me, in my heart of hearts, it was a turning point. Before that,

Chernihiv had also been bombed mercilessly. A youth center, a DIY store, and a children's dental clinic had been destroyed. At that moment, I realized that libraries, stadiums, monuments, and stores weren't important. What mattered were the people. And they died.

Chornovil Street is a residential area. There were no military targets nearby. (This phrase about the absence of military targets seems so well-worn already. We've all heard it too many times, even though we know that the Russians don't care what they bomb. They don't wage war by the book. And killing civilians is perfectly normal for them. For us, it's appalling and we shed tears over the losses, tears of anger and amazement. For them, it's no different from taking a sip of water or spitting at their feet). On Chornovil Street, there were high-rise apartments. There was also a pharmacy and a store, with people queuing in front of them. According to estimates by Human Rights Watch and Amnesty International, around forty-seven people were killed and eighteen injured that day.

***

Chernihiv was under enemy fire. I kept running because of the alarm. One day, some colleagues from Odesa wrote to me to ask me to report live on the situation in the city. Of course, I agreed. I really wanted to work. And if I could make myself useful in this way, it made sense to seize the opportunity. We connected by video. That's when the air raid alarm went off. As communication wasn't good enough in the cellar, I moved to the landing between the apartments, which I thought was the best option. I recounted the incessant bombardments and the successes of our soldiers. Essentially, I took a summary from official sources and supplemented it with my personal observations. Finally, I was asked if public transport was working. And that's when I realized that people outside our city didn't understand just how critical the situation was. The minibuses and trolleybuses had stopped running at midday on February 24. Because of the constant risk of being shot at. After the first day of the full-scale invasion, public transport was no longer an option, as the situation was so dangerous. I remember being so surprised by this question that I wrote an article about it on a social network. And then people wrote to me in the comments that Chernihiv wasn't talked about enough. Too little is known about Chernihiv.

To be honest, I didn't take the risk of running and filming for one simple reason: I didn't have a press card. Chernihiv is a small town. And after working in the media for about seven years, I simply didn't need one. A lot of people knew me and, at the time of the invasion, I was a presenter and I wasn't doing

any reporting for which I would have needed a press card. I worked for an evening entertainment show and the content I produced was accordingly light and entertaining.

Shortly before February 24, I was preparing a program on how to register as a woman in the army. Indeed, certain professional groups had to do so, so that the state would have an overview of who it could rely on in extreme cases. This does not mean that these women will be sent to the front. It simply means that, in an absolute emergency, they can be asked to do what they have been trained to do. This is the case for women working in communications, metrology, or finance. The same applies to journalists. I filmed a report for the show and also had myself recorded. It felt right and important. I really wanted to do it. But I didn't get the call.

I informed my colleagues in other countries about what was happening here. I made a few small contributions to the current situation, which were then used for a production in a Polish theater. I also wrote messages on Facebook, but they were more motivational than informative. Not a day went by when I wasn't annoyed by the fact that what I was doing didn't even deserve the name of work. At least, that's how I felt. I knew that I could actually control the fear, that I could film, and that I could also produce contributions in a hurry. I think I had this psychological problem that's very common in our town—the feeling that you're not doing enough or that you're not doing anything at all.

***

One day, I learned of the death of my friend Iryna, who was a photographer. She was killed by Russian soldiers who dropped a bomb on a school. The school was home to a volunteer center that distributed food and collected clothes for people in need. Ira was a very active and cheerful person. She was always positive and shared her optimism with others. She was very creative and imaginative. She came to school with her husband and son, wanting to help. Her husband survived, not her. When I heard about it, I didn't believe it. It simply couldn't be true. Ira, radiant and smiling, could not have died under the rubble of the school. Then I saw the Instagram photos of her daughter, who was desperately looking for her mother. The young girl was abroad and constantly striving for information.

Ira's story is just one of many. According to some reports, over seven hundred people died during the active fighting in the city. However, this figure remains approximate, according to the lowest estimate. Some died instantly, others under the rubble. Each death is our common pain, our common sorrow. Regardless of whether we knew them or not. We can only take comfort in knowing that they will be with us for as long as we think of them. And we do think of them. And we'll never forget who did this. They were normal people, smiling, dreaming, planning vacations, going to work, and walking in the park on Sundays. They were people like you.

***

When there's a war just outside your window, you think, whether you like it or not, about the value of life. I didn't want to leave. Until the last moment, I thought I could be useful over there. That I belonged there. I don't know why, but I wasn't afraid in Chernihiv. No matter how hard the shooting was, no matter how much information was circulating about the imminent capture of the city, I wasn't afraid. I knew I could die at any moment, but I wasn't afraid. The only thing that worried me was that I might be injured and not receive medical attention, but I tried not to think about it. I wasn't afraid because there were a lot of our soldiers in Chernihiv. And I felt protected.

My mother was in my hometown, seventy-four kilometers away. At first, she held out, but around March 8, she collapsed. She cried on the phone and asked me to leave. Anywhere, but away from the fighting.

There were no evacuations to speak of in Chernihiv. People left at their own risk. Some made it, others did not. Some were killed by shellfire or directly by the enemy. There were people—incredible people—who organized the evacuation of civilians themselves. These volunteers are other Chernihiv heroes. They brought out old people, women, and children in their private vehicles. And on the way back, they brought humanitarian aid and medicines.

My mother got in touch with someone who did this kind of evacuation. This person worked with the Red Cross, I later found out. To make sure I went, my mother told me that my school friend and her husband were still in Chernihiv. Their child was in our hometown—they'd taken him to stay with his grandparents for a week. But now they were stuck in Chernihiv and didn't know how to reach their son. When I suggested they return together, they agreed. So I was responsible for other people.

So the three of us set off. When we got to the starting point, a missile crashed into a nearby house. People immediately ran away, even my friends. I just stood there, as if nothing had happened. The whistle of shells and the sound of rockets had become something quite normal for me. After all, it's war. And in wartime, it's like that. When we got into the minibus, the passengers started to panic. They shouted at us to get in now, that there was gunfire. I replied coolly that shots were fired every day. And hysteria wouldn't help.

The day I arrived was my mother's birthday. And she stopped crying. It was worth sacrificing my ambitions and hopes.

***

After I left Chernihiv, there was no water. The enemy had damaged the water supply system. It was impossible to repair. Vodokanal employees brought in drinking water from tanks and poured it into five-liter buckets and plastic bottles. As they couldn't reach all the districts, the inhabitants had to take care of the water themselves. They fetched water from the river and collected rainwater. The sewage system no longer worked either. So people dug toilets in the courtyards. All they had to do was cut holes between the buildings to get to the toilet. Yes, it's probably not the most pleasant communication, but it was reality.

A few days after my departure, the bridge over the Desna was destroyed. It was the main link with Kyiv. The people of Chernihiv were trapped. Without food or water and under constant bullet fire.

***

And then, during the war, I was forced to learn to fear after all. One morning, my mother received a phone call saying that the Russians had entered our town. It was an acquaintance of hers. She shouted into the phone that several tanks and armored vehicles were driving through the streets. There were no soldiers in our town at the time. They were defending Chernihiv. We were on our own. However, it wasn't quite as many had said. The Russians came to us in two cars. They took our mayor and a few men. Then they left. But the mere fact that they were in town scared me. At the time, there was still no news from Butsha or Irpin, but I suspected that this might be the case wherever there were occupiers. I was very afraid of being humiliated in front of my family and having to endure physical violence. My mother wanted to hide me somewhere, but that made me uncomfortable too. Why should I hide in my own home? What had I done? I decided that I would defend myself if the situation became really critical, and I thought of a way to do it without harming my family. I hid my phone in a safe place, as I had saved many business contacts on it.

About a week later, the Russians brought our mayor back and left. He had been beaten, but he was alive. The others were not brought back. We don't know what happened to them. I've been vigilant all week and it's a good thing I've been relatively calm. If I'd been scared, it wouldn't have done me any good in the end.

When I think back on it now, I'm amazed that I wasn't scared during the blockade of Chernihiv, which was mercilessly bombarded by planes and artillery. But the thought of occupation scared me. I think you understand why if you've seen the photos of Butsha. Or if you've heard about the village of Yahidne in the Chernihiv region. There, over three hundred people, including children and the elderly, were held prisoner in a narrow cellar. No food, no water. No possibility of sleeping in a comfortable position. They had to stay next to the bodies of those who had died from lack of oxygen.

I've collected some of these stories myself. It's very difficult to talk to people who have suffered violence. When they talk about the nightmare, they sometimes relive it all over again. The world needs to know about this. Any war crimes committed against Ukrainian citizens must be recorded and made public. If there is justice in this world, if there are laws in this world, and if human rights are respected, Russia must be held accountable for everything it has done in our country. For every child who died. For every woman raped. For every soldier who has been tortured and mistreated. For every stone of our homes destroyed. And for every tear we shed.

***

When the Russians were driven out of the region, I decided to return to Chernihiv. Life wasn't the same as before, but it went on. I soon went back to work and started shooting reports for the TV news. Entertaining evening shows were out of the question. I had to walk to the office, as public transport had not yet resumed. And every day, on the way, I saw destroyed buildings, shell-damaged trees, and people with indescribable weariness in their eyes.

***

Every day, I realize that I could die, and I accept this fact quietly, without needing pity or compassion.

I'm writing these last lines in Ukrainian because the most important thing I have is Ukrainian. And because, despite my Russian-speaking origins, it has become my everyday language.

I still hope to be mobilized to make myself useful to my country. I absolutely want to do something useful and I feel motivated, after all, we have to make an effort now, there may not be another chance.

It was difficult to write this text. First of all, I don't think my story is particularly interesting. I simply survived the active fighting at Chernihiv. Secondly, it's hard to admit certain things, like that I'm terribly afraid of an occupation. Or

that I assume that I didn't fulfill my mission because I didn't take the risk of working without a press card. But I know that I could die at any moment. And if there's an opportunity to leave something, like this text, for example, I should seize it. This way, I have the chance to continue living at least on the pages of this book. I'm not going to die like that. I'm fighting and I'll continue to fight, I'll do everything in my power to ensure that the victory of my Ukraine comes as soon as possible. For I am from Chernihiv, the city of legendary resistance.

P.S. The war is extremely horrible, disgusting, and dirty. The Ukrainians did not start this war, but we have had to accept it. We are fighting for our loved ones, for our lives, for our right to be independent and free. We are defending our home, all of us.

If you only know about war from the news, movies, books, and other publications, I'll give you a word of advice. Appreciate everything you have. At every opportunity, tell your loved ones how much you love and appreciate them. Take the time to have coffee with your friends. Travel with them. Don't be afraid to make your dreams come true. Because one day, it could all come to an end. Someone might decide you're living too well and need to be "rescued" from that situation.

Ukraine is desperately fighting this someone. And I believe we will win. I believe we will stop this giant monster who brings only death, destruction, and evil.

After all, we understand only too well the importance of peace.

And at what price this peace is achieved?

[Author's note: After writing this letter, Dina was mobilized. She has been fighting in the Ukrainian armed forces for almost two years and has vowed to do so until the end of the war, until her country is victorious.]

By Hannah Marholina

Date of birth: April 4, 2001
From: Melitopol
Profession: Fashion designer
In Bali at the start of the invasion

December 5, 2022

My name is Khanna Marholina, and I come from Melitopol, Ukraine. This means that for me, war has been going on for nine years already.

But on the day of February 24, 2022, the enemy appeared as obvious as the difference between black and white. I heard my mother crying like a little kitten, moaning while I was sitting on the terrace of our hotel room in Ubud, Bali, where we had arrived about two weeks before.

I had to leave the city where I worked to be able to support myself for the two previous years, Milan, because my visa-free period expired, and I was forced to leave Italy for three months. I was not feeling well, either in my body or soul, because since the end of January, I haven't left my bed, and have only been able to lay down with a cheek stuck to the pillow, listening to news about a possible invasion of Ukraine. So, my mom decided to take me there, where she had already been for some months, so I could recover a bit and because she was scared to let me go back to Kyiv while the news was spreading all over the world.

"12:55 Takeoff of 3TU-MKS RF from military airfield 'Engels.' Friends, activity of enemy aviation, massive air raid alert is possible."

These were the notifications on my phone. Humans get used to everything.

Since I was eleven, I got to know a lot of Russian people who are working in fashion and art, the music industry and science, and psychoanalysis. Also, since I studied philosophy, I've always been following the situation of human rights and freedom in Russia. For me it has always been very important; nonetheless, I've always been terrified by the horrific events there. I love diversity, I share humanist principles, and it was impossible not to have my heart constrict after hearing of violence and persecution towards LGBT communities, atheists, all kinds of illegal persecution of opposition to the Government, the everyday practice of incriminating innocents, and much more.

After the invasion started, I was spending my days in a very realistic nightmare, or rather a sleep paralysis. You see yourself constantly being killed or followed by a monster, who's standing beside your bed, but you're not able to move.

I felt pity for these vulnerable people, I felt like it was a dark muddy monster that is the main threat to innocent people all around the world, not only in Russia, and which modernity has to fight against. And on that day of February 24, this mud spread all over my motherland.

Two days before the war started we were driving in a car with Mom, deciding where to go after our trip, and she said she might come back to Ukraine to continue our seasonal family business on the seaside and I went into tears. I don't remember crying badly. I was so scared and overwhelmed by what was surrounding us on that crowded island, on foreign land lives away from the motherland, miles away from the threat of war, powerless to do anything about what was going to happen.

I remember twelve-year-old me sitting in an empty cold bath, experiencing teenage dysmorphia, and thinking about the fact that I would not be able to go to a good university. I realized it pretty well. Because Russian soldiers invaded Donbas and occupied Crimea, and we lost our income. My family's hotel was placed very close to the front line, very close to the highway to Crimea, and additionally, we had mostly Russian and Belarussian clients. People were scared to come here, and Russians were scared that they would be in danger in Ukraine. One hotel on the highway in Melitopol we had to sell in 2015 because no one was coming anymore. Ukrainians stopped going to Russia. Russians were scared that they would not be safe in Ukraine and people would hate them here, like we are Nazis. Like we became Nazis in one year.

My family is my mother's family. We are Jewish; our great-grandfather was a rabbi who was killed in Dnipropetrovs'k. When persecution of Jewish people started, he moved his family (my grandfather's mother and their kids) to Melitopol. Part of my family was repatriated to Israel. Once my grandfather, my favorite human being, with a gentle heart, gifted me a little family treasure. It was a little book with a nice shape. Extremely well made, I thought maybe it was a piece with photo cards. What was in my hands were handprinted photos and descriptions of locations in Auschwitz translated into five languages. It was a little tiny thing, maybe five by five cm, but it weighed tons and tons. It was very heavy. I could not keep it with me, so I gave it to the "Library of Fine Arts."

How does it feel to be Ukrainian and Jewish nowadays? Cursed? I wouldn't say so. It makes you remember that we didn't do enough to ensure the power of law and the protection of human rights. The world community hasn't done enough to prevent these events. It should be totally impossible for anyone to have such a big military power, and if someone has it, they should not be able to use it. One must underline that the Russian opposition was translating the narrative about their criminal government and systematical violation of human rights and freedoms, untransparent elections, and dictatorship. And what had we done with it? Nothing. No reaction from the world community. No actions. I have been following up on it for years.

Permissiveness for the Russian government to translate its propaganda and spread hostile messages about Ukraine and Western society has continued for years. Actions for peace must have a preventative character, not a reactive one. As we really well know now, it was too late. Incredibly late.

I think it was in 2017. I couldn't face the reality that this event took place. But it did. And it happened again.

As Hannah Arendt said, evil is banal.

About six months after the war started, the nephew of my stepfather who lived in Donets'k was trapped in a wet, two meter earth pit because he answered in a way the Russians didn't like at the checkpoint. He was fourteen, he spent two days there, and they broke eight of his ribs. He arrived at our home, safe, but badly beaten. That was only a start. After many years I started to have flashbacks about these checkpoints this summer. I remember them; it was really scary when you are a teen and you see these men with guns, and my mom had to stop the car so they can make sure that we could go. I almost forgot about it but my memories were fresh, with a taste of cold and grey school days, illuminated with the impression made by my teacher of Ukrainian and the start of Ukrainization in schools. It brought into my education process a very pleasant detail. I was always mesmerized by Ukrainian culture and literature, so I was happy about it. Municipal facilities were colored yellow and blue and it was beautiful. Anyway, dark days, very dark days, when we were on lessons knowing that two hundred km from us our people were dying in battles, in cold trenches, for our freedom, for our dignity, and the possibility to learn our history and choose our future. For Russian imperialistic culture, it was never possible. They always tried to erase our historical memory, our identity, and our culture. They tried to change what we think about ourselves. They have been calling us Nazis for at least one hundred years already. Why? Because we are the real posterity of Kyiv Rus. Because Ukrainian artists, writers, painters, musicians, and composers are the ones whom Russians appropriated and called Russians, exactly the ones who are called "representatives of great Russian culture." Of course, this answer is too simple. We can give tons and tons of these answers and all of them will be true.

Two days before, we also had a meeting with my mom's English teacher. She was Russian and they were discussing the news. She said that Putin is rationally afraid and that she is scared that NATO puts their weapons eighty km from Russia. She said as well that she respects him because he annulled her debt to the bank. I told my mother that I was not gonna meet this woman anymore and that I was not gonna talk to my mother as well if she did so. My mother was mad. Also on the 24th, this friend had a birthday. Of course, no one went there but she dared to try to push us to come.

About a week after February 24, I didn't sleep. Every couple of seconds news was arriving. Air strikes, bombs, rockets. My task was to help my underaged male friends to evacuate as fast as possible from Ukraine. For this, I needed to find a car that could take them to any city far from Kyiv at first, and then to Lviv, and from there to the Polish border. Sounds easy, but it was impossible. I was desperately trying to find a car everywhere and the saddest place was telegram groups with people like me. But they were in Ukraine, I was in Bali. They had kids and grandparents, cats, and dogs. No one could propose a ride. From what I saw, they weren't succeeding either. I couldn't close my eyes for a minute, I knew that it was my duty to find at least one car. On highways were billions of cars—heavy traffic. In some of them, Russians arrived already, and people were dying with this absurd death being shot from tanks or mine explosions.

To survive you needed to have a car full of gas and know a highway controlled by Ukrainians without Russian tanks. We tried to share as much information between us as possible. Which way is faster and safer, where there is no way anymore due to explosions, where you can buy gas for the car? I felt so connected and so proud of my friends' community. We were together and we were strong.

Some of my friends decided to stay home and only go to the bomb shelter, not panicking, not wanting to leave their homes. Some of them were making stories crying and yelling with the sound of explosions, gunshots, and people screaming in the background. Everyone was full of hate.

I couldn't cry. I was not crying. I didn't have time for that. I was constantly checking on my friends from two phones and one laptop. Thinking of what sound could describe what happened at that time. Maybe short rare breaths or maybe rare silent tears falling on an always-lit-up screen. The worst thing was coming. The Russians hit communication towers and then the real nightmare started. I didn't know if my loved ones were alive. My grandpa had no food. One time when they hit the communications in Melitopol and occupied the city we didn't hear from him for three days and no one could check if he was okay. These days were the worst days of my life. After the connection was back, he called us in tears crying, saying how he loved us and how scared he was that he would never hear our voices again. Melitopol has been occupied since the first days of the war. People there are being raped, kidnapped, and killed. Their bodies were found sometimes just downstairs buried in their own courts. Kids, especially young girls, and men. Innocent people are killed by ignorance, thirst for blood, permissiveness, right to power, and greed. Every day I live with the understanding that my grandfather who is my closest relative lives surrounded by every kind of sadism.

If you don't know who you are, where you come from, where your roots are and what is your goal, and you never even wanted to know about that, then committing a massacre is not a question of morals. It becomes a paragraph in the schedule. There is no place for honor. No place either for solidarity, and soldier dignity.

When the reality is so grotesque, you will not react to it like in a dramatic movie. It takes your speech away and feels like there is no need to say anything. A speechless reality that makes you deaf by how loud it is.

They came to the holy lands of my motherland to play their music on a victory parade. Fascists came to occupy Ukraine and celebrate the victory of fascism. They took their musical instruments!

Why we can't surrender? Because in imperialistic politics we pay taxes with our freedom. And we are a very freedom-loving nation. The Ukrainian idea is to have an equal society with people of all races, nationalities, and religions, gender, having equal rights and freedoms, respecting the Ukrainian constitution, and honoring Ukrainian culture and history. If we surrender, Ukraine won't be Ukraine anymore.

The first days of the full-scaled invasion I was preoccupied with my LGBTQ friends. If they torture straight people, what they would do with them? What made the fear unbearable was that Russians were barbarous before the war started. War, permissiveness, ignorance, and absence of empathy and discipline summarized with the poor and extremely poor Russian way of living, as well because of their corrupted criminal government that made them see the possibility of going to war for money as acceptable and sometimes the only available option to make money. What could they do to occupied territories? And now we know it. And the one thing I do know is that my fear was justified. The world faced the massacres done on occupied territories by people who consciously denied the possibility for oneself to regret, to share common values and any kind of sensitivity. I am proving this for myself every day when I watch interviews with Russian soldiers.

When we win the war, when it comes to an end, when we have documented this range of all kinds of pure sadism, we will ask ourselves why they died, those who fell. And it won't be answered; I doubt someone has an answer.

About language.

My mother tongue is Russian. In Melitopol where I am from people mostly speak Russian. But not all of them. My grandmother spoke Ukrainian; she sang me Ukrainian lullabies and we prayed in Ukrainian. I always spoke Ukrainian freely and enjoyed Ukrainian literature, and that made me move for the first year of university to L'viv, a Ukrainian-speaking city twenty-four hours away on a train, to enjoy the charming Ukrainian culture more. In 2015 we did a performance with my friend, a poet from Kharkiv, a Russian-speaking city bordering Russia, reading the same book on the same page but in Ukrainian and Russian at the same time. That's how it was before. We thought that it didn't matter; we were naive. He moved to L'viv, so I moved there one year later. Now he is mad at me if I post some old songs by Russian artists. I don't do it anymore. I don't post any text in Russian. My mom started to post in Ukrainian even though she never spoke it. Why? Because she was studying in school when Ukraine was a part of the Soviet Union. And Ukrainian wasn't a necessary thing to learn, in Ukraine. Why? Because there was no goal to teach people their own language. It had to be forgotten or at least Russified. As a result, it was wounded and crippled as a result of endless repressions of those who tried to cultivate authentic Ukrainian language, culture, and identity. Still, we have it and we have defended it.

Even though now death by ambush, by mine fragments, and by missiles falling in your kitchen, has become our normal life.

When something like this happens to your nation, to your motherland, you lose the need to track time. It doesn't matter when summer is coming and what will be next year. You are constantly waiting for an end, without strictly realizing what is the end, and if it can come at all if the streets of your city are covered with dead. If the road that goes to your school is smashed by tank tracks. The bloodless world is still not even just a dream, that is so fantastic, I doubt that someone can have even a dream about it. A unicorn seems more real.

I want you to understand my position correctly. I am against war and violence. I am against death for a plot of land. I am against cultivating rage and hate related to Russians. But the truth is they came to our land with weapons. They came to steal the present and past from people. This war is not a war for territories. We are defending ourselves from pure terror and fighting only for the chance to save our dignity, freedom, and right to choose our future. We don't want to be Russified anymore. What has to happen—they have to go home. They choose fighting rather than working, torture rather than help, and that is what is creating the difference between us.

I hope there will be a place for kindness again. I wish Russians to return their hearts that became stones and remember that violence was never a real power and truth.

By Kateryna Iakovlenko

Date of birth: November 27, 1989
From: Rovenky, Luhansk region
Profession: Visual culture researcher and writer
In Irpin at the start of the large-scale invasion; escaped with her sister and niece to Vienna on March 10, 2022.

June 27, 2022*
*Russia continues its offensive on the eastern and southern fronts. At least three people were killed in Kharkiv. Earlier in the day, Russia launched a rocket attack on a shopping mall in Kremenchuk where people were staying. Some people were killed and others were wounded.
A letter to those who will come after us.

This text should be a letter, but a letter without an addressee.

It's a letter addressed to an unknown future, to people I don't know, perhaps to relatives or acquaintances.

But I don't want to address future generations with abstract generalizations and blurred images. I want to see before me brave people who defended their country against the Russian war and all other forms of fascism. A generation that has withstood all the hardships of war and post-war. A generation capable of making the right decisions. Empathetic and supportive. Strong and above all: a generation that values the freedom of others to live.

I'm writing this text at the end of June. The blazing sun is far from friendly, burning everything around it. But unlike back home, in the steppes of Luhansk, here in Vienna there are plenty of parks where you can escape the stifling summer heat. The only thing you can't escape is the war. Now, all thoughts revolve around it. Mornings and evenings are filled not with the scent of blooming herbs and trees, but with images of bombed-out cities where life used to be good. This summer has crept so insidiously into our lives, depriving Ukrainians of the joy of smelling spring, enjoying everyday life and finally breathing life into their lungs. This year, spring has been marked by blood, fear, and violence. And every time a missile hits a block of flats or a kindergarten, my heart sinks.

War is undoubtedly horrible, but as I've lived through it myself, those are just empty words to me. It's not just horrible in principle but in detail. For some, this experience is a step towards a future that can be changed. But for most, it's a tragedy full of trauma and suffering. The loss of home, the loss of family and friends—even if they are still alive, and the forced severance of relationships with them can be no less tragic.

During war, words lose their meaning, but at the same time, words help us to move forward. There's no recipe for keeping your mind sharp and clear. There's nothing wrong with strong feelings, the important thing is to be able to live with them. Knowing how to live with yourself. Even if you sometimes have to live with yourself in shelters, in overcrowded emergency housing for displaced people and refugees, hundreds of kilometers from home, and share space not with people you love, but with people you don't even know.

In this war, we are alone.

But we're together. I live this war through my own experience as a woman, of course. Through the physical experience of pain, tragedy, and loss. Through the experience of my sister, who is in the EU for the first time in her life with a young child. And although she's already got all the papers, she can't find accommodation or work. This is also the case for other mothers who find themselves alone with their children, who are just as traumatized by the war. They have to explain to their children why they have suddenly had to leave their home and can no longer see their dad, family, and friends, or play with their own toys. How do you explain to a four-year-old what war is, and why one neighboring country is trying to destroy another? Why are missiles still flying over Kyiv, and what does it mean? And when will it all end, and how? We have to explain everything to children, even the things we don't want to tell ourselves. That's why we have to find the words and have the courage to explain and speak out. And sometimes it's a pity we can't shoot back with words—because if someone aims a precision weapon at your loved ones, you'll want to scream and defend them. Sometimes with your own body.

The further away you are from home—which has literally become everything—the more you feel connected to the country where you were born. Things that were once banal become surprisingly important, and in this banality lurk warmth and comfort. This is why the materiality of war is so insidious: you can lose everything at once, but you can also gain everything. Things that were previously of no particular importance take on the greatest value. And among these things is assistance. When I look at the experiences of women, my friends, who have found themselves alone in other contexts and in foreign cities, with children and backpacks, I see how this solicitude materializes and gives them strength.

War isn't something that happens with a scythe and a black jacket. It's what catches people in a queue outside a bakery or in a store where they want to buy flowers. War comes early in the morning, when everyone is asleep, because at dawn it feels the power over the strongest. But life is always stronger than death.

In this war, all experiences have their value, and their meaning. And however hard the memories of war may be, they must be preserved with the same care, for it is they that can protect us from other wars.

Preserve your memories.

We are all we have.

By Emily Channell-Justice

Date of birth: August 2, 1986
From: Falling Waters, West Virginia, USA
Profession: Anthropologist; Director of the Temerty Contemporary Ukraine Program, Ukrainian Research Institute, Harvard University
In Somerville, Massachusetts (USA) at the start of the invasion

October 10, 2022

On a beautiful May day in 2022, I had plans to visit a friend and fellow anthropologist in Warsaw. Marta and I had previously spent an afternoon together walking around Praga, one of the city's historic neighborhoods. Marta, whose expertise is in religion, pilgrimage, and ideas of "home," pointed out small courtyard chapels within housing complexes, with unique and colorful details added by residents. She'd left her home and her job in Kyiv just weeks before and, despite her many years of research experience in Poland, she was clearly struggling to adjust to life there when her mother was still at home in Kyiv, constantly living under the threat of Russian bombs.

Later that month, Marta and I made plans to go on a long walk around another part of the city. But when I met her on the tram, she told me that Liza, an old schoolmate of hers, was arriving from Kyiv later that day with her eleven-year-old daughter. Liza spoke English, but she'd never been to Poland and didn't know Polish at all. Marta wanted to meet them at the train station and help them navigate the city so they could spend the night somewhere safe. They arrived at Warsaw's western train station with a suitcase and a heavy backpack each, wearing baseball caps and comfortable clothes. Liza hadn't really planned to leave Ukraine, but she knew some other Ukrainians in Germany, so she and her daughter finally made the decision and took an evacuation train to the Polish border, planning to go on to Germany from there.

When she first arrived, Liza seemed surprisingly composed. She knew that the Expo Center in Warsaw was hosting Ukrainians for free, so she planned on getting a bed there for the night. But navigating the Polish welcome system wasn't easy—there was information and hot food at the train station, but the bus to the Expo Center didn't have a regular schedule. Plus, there would have to be enough passengers, or else the bus would wait for more people, and Liza didn't really want to wait around the train station for hours. She was afraid for her daughter, who looked much older than her eleven years. She told me, quietly, that she had heard stories of Ukrainian women getting kidnapped and raped by taxi drivers in Poland, so she only wanted to use public transportation. On top of that, she was concerned about whether there would be enough security at the Expo Center to protect a single woman and her daughter.

Marta mobilized her network to find a host for Liza and her daughter—a friend of a friend (another anthropologist) could take them in for a few days. But Liza didn't want to impose. She was afraid of what might happen at the Expo Center, but it was a free resource for Ukrainians. Staying at someone's home was another story. Marta and I tried to convince her that this host wouldn't have offered if she didn't want to help, and that many Poles were opening their homes to Ukrainians. Finally, the promise of breakfast and a hot shower—and a safer place for her daughter—made Liza accept the offer. But the difficulty in making what seemed to me like an obvious decision showed how much escaping the war was weighing on Liza.

Once Liza had finally made her decision, Marta turned to me and said, "I'm sorry, Emily, that we didn't get to have our walk, but I'm going to help Liza get to this woman's apartment." I wanted to support Liza, but I didn't want to be in the way, since Marta knew her way around the city, spoke Polish, and could help Liza navigate Warsaw's complex but comprehensive public transport system. I pushed 50 zloty into Liza's hand and told Marta to make sure that she didn't try to give it back, and I hugged Marta and Liza and wished them luck. A few hours later, I got a message from Marta. It said, "Liza was crying all the way in the metro, saying how kind you were, and that she has never taken money from unknown people." Like most people, Liza wasn't used to people doing her favors and in any normal circumstance, she would have never taken that money. For me, it was the least I could do.

Meeting Liza and her daughter impacted me like almost nothing else I saw in Warsaw. I spent weeks there, packing free groceries, helping people find clothes to fit them and their children at a free shop, and dishing out hot food at the central train station. I spoke to refugees from Kyiv, Ivano-Frankivs'k, Odesa, Kharkiv, Zaporizhzhia, and Donets'k. I listened to stories of people hiding in basements with their children while bombs fell and cried with them when they told me how grateful they were to the American volunteers who handed out bottles of water at the border. But for some reason, meeting Liza brought the war home to me in a painfully personal way. I felt viscerally that it could have been me in her place.

Women like Marta, Liza, and the others I talked to reflect the diverse origins of Ukrainians. They are active participants in building a Ukrainian identity that is inclusive of everyone living in Ukraine but which is also, most importantly, distinct from Russia and from Russian identity. Despite Ukraine's reputation as a conservative country with a poor record on gender equality, the reality is that women have been active participants in Ukrainian society, politics, and culture for centuries.

What Does It Mean to be Ukrainian?

What does it mean to be Ukrainian today? Like most modern identities, the answer isn't always clear. As we have seen from the letters included in this book, Ukrainians see themselves in diverse ways. Some reflect deeply on their identity as Ukrainian and what it means to them to be part of contemporary Ukraine. Others simply lived their lives with Ukrainian citizenship. But since February 24, 2022, all of them have had to contend with Russia's threat to the very existence of Ukraine. Some have switched to speaking Ukrainian; some have become global advocates for their country. Some have experienced discrimination because of their connections with Russia. Many have left Ukraine and are now settled abroad, at least for the time being. Many others remain in Ukraine, participating however they can in the war effort.

While there is no single way to be Ukrainian, it has become clear that Russia, and in particular, President Putin, underestimated the extent to which people living in Ukraine would fight for their country. Perhaps he should have known, because for those of us who have spent extended periods of time in Ukraine in the last decade, we were not surprised to see the Ukrainian response. Particularly since 2014, Ukrainians have understood that they are the drivers of society and politics. In 2013, when pro-Russian president Viktor Yanukovych refused to sign an Association Agreement with the European Union, Ukrainians came into the streets of cities across the country (most notably in mass protests in the capital city of Kyiv and throughout western Ukraine, but also including cities in eastern Ukraine, such as Kharkiv, Donets'k, and even in Crimea). In February 2014, after one hundred protesters were killed by pro-regime forces, Yanukovych fled the country, and a new era was ushered in by these Euromaidan protests.

Before delving more deeply into women's roles during wartime in contemporary Ukraine, it is first necessary to explore how women have lived in Ukrainian society throughout history. Despite negative stereotypes, Ukrainian women have been important players in various social and political movements, and scholarship on gender is a robust field within Ukraine.

Women's Participation in Ukrainian Society

Ukraine is known for having limited social roles for women. Famed gender scholar Oksana Kis has described these limited options as the "Barbie or *berehynia*" model.[1] The first option indicates that women are only seen as objects of desire, reduced to their sexuality and beauty. Indeed, Ukraine has earned a

---

[1] See her 2005 article, "Choosing Without Choice: Predominant Models of Femininity in Contemporary Ukraine," in *Gender Transitions in Russia and Eastern Europe*, ed. Madeline Hurd, Helen Carlback, and Sara Rastback (Stockholm: Gondolin, 2005). See also work by Solomea Pavlychko and Tamara Zlobina.

reputation as a destination for sex tourism. The *berehynia* model, on the other hand, comes from a pre-Christian image of a nurturing "hearth-mother" who protects the family and, through it, the nation.[2] Both images of women rely on naturalizing ideas that women are caretakers, mothers, and wives, and that they are only part of the domestic and private worlds.

Certainly, life for women in Ukraine has always been more complex than just these two options. Women have always fought for their place in society, and they have taken active roles in national movements throughout the country's fight for its self-determination.[3] Ukrainian women also served as combatants in and after World War II, famously participating in the anti-Soviet nationalist organizations, the Organization of Ukrainian Nationalists (OUN) and the Ukrainian Insurgent Army (UPA) in the 1940s and 1950s.[4]

Women's roles in contemporary Ukraine are also strongly influenced by the experience of state socialism. Soviet communist ideology promised gender equality and freeing women from domestic burdens, in particular by encouraging their emancipation through their entrance into the labor force. Women were granted the right to vote in the Soviet Union in 1917, and feminist activists founded the *Zhenotdel*, or Women's Department, of the Communist Party, to ensure discussion of women's equality. The USSR passed legislation to allow for divorce, maternity leave, and state-funded childcare, as well as the legalization of abortion.

However, despite these seemingly positive changes for women in the early twentieth century, over the course of the existence of the USSR, gender equality was not a reality. Instead of women being freed from domestic responsibilities because of their participation in the labor force, they were more likely to experience a "double burden"—they were expected to participate in labor outside the home, as well as raise families inside the home. Additionally, many scholars have pointed out that gendered divisions of labor continued to exist in the Soviet Union. Fields dominated by women (such as education and medicine) were related to biological assumptions about women's caretaking abilities, for instance.

---

[2] Marian Rubchak has written extensively about the significance of the *berehynia* as a model for women and even for feminism in contemporary Ukraine.

[3] Scholar Martha Bohachevsky-Chomiak's historical research on women's organizations in Ukraine between 1880 and the mid-twentieth century shows that women were active participants in nation-building projects in Ukraine at this time.

[4] Oksana Kis and Marta Havryshko have both written extensive academic research on the participation of women in these organizations.

By the mid-1930s, Joseph Stalin introduced new, pronatalist policies designed to encourage (or force) women to have more children: abortion was recriminalized, divorce became difficult to obtain, and Stalin declared the "women's question" to have been solved. The Zhenotdel was abolished, so women had little chance to push gender-based questions within the Soviet political structure. Stalin further masterminded the policies that created a famine across Ukraine, known as the *Holodomor*, which killed some four million people and destroyed the foundations of the Ukrainian national movement. Of course, these policies could not crush Ukrainian national identity, and dissidents fought for Ukraine's independence throughout the next decades of Soviet rule.

For women, Soviet gender equality policies became one of the many unfulfilled promises of the state. Thus, when Ukraine became independent from the Soviet Union in 1991, scholars studying gender and activists hoping to establish feminist groups in Ukraine (as well as in other newly independent post-Soviet republics) noticed a lack of interest, and sometimes even hostility, toward feminism and gender politics. Extensive scholarship on women's non-governmental organizations in Ukraine and beyond has shown the disconnect between western funding organizations' priorities and the needs of women on the ground. In other words, many feminist NGOs that were established in Ukraine in the 1990s were often not actually listening to Ukrainian women and what they said they needed, preferring instead to pursue their own areas of interest.[5]

Yet, robust debates around feminism and gender politics have developed in Ukraine in the thirty-three years of its independence. Several Ukrainian academics established schools of feminist literary criticism, drawing on a combination of European and North American theoretical traditions and the historical trend of women's participation in Ukrainian political life described earlier.[6] Feminist and gender-based activism saw a resurgence in the 2000s, including, most visibly, the topless protest group FEMEN, whose participants sometimes protested against gender inequality and discrimination but, more often, used their topless protests to draw attention to unrelated issues.[7]

---

[5] For research based in Ukraine, see Sarah Phillips and Alexandra Hrycak. For research based in Russia, see Julie Hemment and Janet Johnson. See also Kristen Ghodsee for research on Bulgaria.

[6] Solomea Pavlychko and Irina Zherebkina are the best known feminist academics from this time period.

[7] Whether or not FEMEN is actually a feminist group has gotten extensive treatment among feminist academics both inside and outside of Ukraine.

Throughout the 2000s, Ukrainian politics was extremely male dominated. In the early 2000s, only 5% of members of Parliament were women, and this number stayed under 10% until 2014. The most prominent female political figure throughout this time was Yulia Tymoshenko, who served as prime minister in 2005 and again from 2007-2010. Known for embracing traditional Ukrainian clothing and braided hairstyle, her rise to power was similar to her male counterparts. She made millions in the gas industry, after which she entered politics in 1996 as a member of Ukraine's Verkhovna Rada (Parliament). She was a key figure in the 2004 Orange Revolution, supporting the pro-western candidate Viktor Yushchenko, for whom she would later become prime minister.

Yulia Tymoshenko is Ukraine's most visible post-independence female political figure. However, she has never been known to campaign for expanded representation of women in government, and she has never taken any stances that could be considered feminist. The Euromaidan protests have almost certainly been more influential on women's participation in activist efforts, as well as in women running for office in growing numbers, than any political figure in Ukraine. Women have taken on key roles in active civil society organizations that have developed in the wake of Euromaidan, such as the Anti-Corruption Action Center, Civil Network OPORA, Crimea SOS, and the Center for Civil Liberties, which was awarded the Nobel Peace Prize in October 2022.[8] And, finally, the number of women in Parliament is increasing. Since 2019, over 20% of the Verkhovna Rada is now made up of women.[9] Out of 423 members overall, this number is still dismally low, and President Volodymyr Zelensky's Cabinet of Ministers features only four women (out of twenty-one ministers). While women are more visible at various levels of government than ever before, they are still underrepresented in positions of power.

Because of martial law imposed in Ukraine since the start of the Russian invasion, men between the ages of eighteen and sixty are not allowed to leave Ukraine without a special dispensation. For the first year of war, most men (aside from key political figures like Dmytro Kuleba, Ukraine's foreign minister), were not allowed to leave the country, so most of Ukraine's representation abroad came from women. In July 2022, Olena Zelenska made the first speech in front of the U.S. Congress by a First Lady. She has continued to appear on a variety of media and to make appeals for support for Ukraine in front of numerous

---

[8] The prize was shared between the Russian human rights organization Memorial and jailed Belarusian activist Ales Bialiatski.
[9] World Bank Group, "Proportion of Seats Held by National Parliaments (%)—Ukraine," accessed October 4, 2024, https://data.worldbank.org/indicator/SG.GEN.PARL.ZS?locations=UA.

audiences. While likely not a role the First Lady expected to take, she has been a recognizable and powerful advocate for Ukraine who will show her constituents that women are effective political actors.

Shifting Social Roles: 2014 and Beyond

But these changes in Ukrainian society did not begin in 2019. The 2013-2014 Euromaidan protests were a definitive moment in Ukraine for many reasons. Women participated in large numbers, though they were often pushed into more "feminine" spaces, such as in kitchens, cooking and distributing food to the men who occupied the tent camp in Kyiv's main square. This was necessary work to sustain the thousands-strong tent camp, but many women wanted to be able to choose how they participated for themselves. One aspect of my research on political activism, which took place during the Euromaidan protests, was to explore how marginalized groups created space to participate in the mass protests. Sometimes they were met with negative responses, but women and feminists were actively finding new ways to be present throughout the protests. They pushed back against the idea that women needed to be protected by men and that kitchens were the only appropriate place for women.

Women were also present at the front lines when the war began in 2014. A sociological research project and documentary film, *Invisible Battalion*, was essential in bringing attention to women's combat roles in the war. The project highlighted the fact that women were participating in combat roles but were not allowed to access the same benefits and treatments as male veterans because their roles were not officially recognized. The project became an advocacy campaign that resulted in a change in Ukrainian legislation that expanded the definition of women's combat roles and established a law to ensure the equal rights of male and female members of the Armed Forces.

Researchers for *Invisible Battalion* have not stopped their work after this legislative success. The second edition of the project, *Invisible Battalion 2.0*, focused on women soldiers' return to civilian life, particularly bringing to light the widespread experience of post-traumatic stress disorder and other mental health concerns. In August 2020, the third edition was launched, focusing on sexual harassment in the Armed Forces, which has already published extensive research material and policy recommendations to improve conditions and reporting.[10]

---

[10] Invisible Battalion, accessed October 4, 2024, https://invisiblebattalion.org/en/home-2/.

At the same time that women in the Armed Forces have received unprecedented and deserved attention, the trend of women filling caretaker roles in response to the war continued, as well. Researchers documented women at the forefront of a variety of responses to the war: organizing supplies for soldiers; taking care of wounded and traumatized soldiers returning from the battlefield; and, as we saw earlier, meeting the hundreds of thousands of displaced people when they arrived in new cities and helping organize and distribute humanitarian aid. Nataliia Stepaniuk's research documented volunteer groups, and more than two thirds of the people she interviewed were women. She argues that the "asymmetrical gender composition of Ukrainian volunteer networks" shows that the war mobilization itself was gendered, with men being expected to take up arms and women expected to stay behind. Stepaniuk noted that women met a variety of needs through volunteer groups, including collecting resources and procuring specific items, as well as providing medical care and emotional support—both to demobilized soldiers and to civilians who had experienced the trauma of the war.[11]

In 2014, during the Euromaidan protests, women's roles were recognized as being behind the scenes. In the years that followed, women continued to do behind the scenes work, but their presence on the battlefield brought renewed attention to all the ways women were mobilizing. Now, in 2022, this mobilization has expanded dramatically in response the renewed Russian invasion. Men and women do whatever they can to help people in need and fight for their country's right to exist.

The Impact of War on Ukrainian Society

Since February 24, 2022, martial law has been in use in Ukraine. This means that men between the ages of eighteen and sixty can be called up to the Armed Forces, and they are not allowed to leave the country without special exceptions (including, for example, a health condition, or if they are the father of three or more children). Because of this martial law, the vast majority of people who have fled Ukraine since the war began have been women and children. Millions of Ukrainians crossed the border to European Union countries in the largest movement of people since World War II. In 2022, Poland received more refugees

---

[11] Nataliia Stepaniuk, "Wartime Civilian Mobilization: Demographic Profile, Motivations, and Pathways to Volunteer Engagement amidst the Donbas War in Ukraine," *Nationalities Papers*, May 13, 2022, 1-18.

than any other country, supporting Ukrainians by providing them a special registration status that allowed them to work and receive medical services and free transportation for several months.

In 2024, the situation in Europe looks quite different. Understanding that the war would continue, many refugees either elected to return to Ukraine to be with their husbands, sons, fathers, and brothers, or they moved elsewhere in Europe and North America for the longer term. Germany is now the country with the highest number of Ukrainian refugees (over 1 million), and millions more Ukrainians who fled in February and March 2022 have already returned to Ukraine. The demographic of refugees outside of Ukraine remains mostly women and children, but there are now larger numbers of internally displaced people, including those who have returned from spending a few months abroad at the start of the war but who cannot return to their homes in Ukraine. Even now, the vast majority of Ukrainians abroad say that want to return to Ukraine as soon as they can and plan to return as soon as the war is over. While it is certainly true that some Ukrainians will resettle abroad permanently, it appears that the majority of refugees see their future in Ukraine.

The society that they return to will be dramatically different than the one they left, however. I spent a month in Kyiv in September of 2021, my first visit since the Covid-19 pandemic. The Ukraine I visited then was a vibrant, European society with a growing economy dominated by tech-sector innovation and young minds. But I was there working on a research project about internally displaced people (IDPs). The war in Ukraine's eastern Donbas region began in 2014, and since then, at least 1.5 million people had been forced to leave that territory to go to another part of Ukraine. The Ukrainian government had tried to establish a department to address the needs of IDPs, but for the most part, there was no unified policy. I talked to volunteers and experts who worked for international organizations, who attempted to create more effective policies to meet the needs of IDPs. It was a complex problem, made more challenging by the fact that Russians still occupied parts of the Donets'k and Luhans'k regions and by the fact that many displaced people still hoped to go home. Their hope was mostly not pinned to a political position—for displaced people and for people living in the occupied territories, economic concerns were a bigger problem than who technically controlled the territory. They wanted stable jobs and stable homes, more than anything.

These priorities will likely be the same when Ukraine wins the war, a lasting peace is established, and people return home. Ukraine will be militarized in new ways following the cessation of hostilities. Even now, we are seeing major shifts in the civilian-military relationship. There is a collapse between what we typically explain as "military" and "humanitarian" responses. There are two related reasons that the line between these two ideas is blurred since February 2022. First, the Ukrainian military's reforms since 2015—which include the legislation introduced after the work of *Invisible Battalion*—led to the integration of the Territorial Defense Forces into the Ukrainian Armed Forces. Previously made up of various groups of volunteers, some created during the Euromaidan protests, the Territorial Defense Forces (Ukr. *Terytorial'na oborona*) only formally became part of the Armed Forces in 2022. When the Russian invasion began in February, massive numbers of volunteers signed up for Territorial Defense units across Ukraine. While many volunteers had previous military experience or training, these units have been responsible for many humanitarian missions, such as the evacuation of civilians from occupied towns and villages.

Relatedly, military actions continue to be what make the delivery and distribution of humanitarian aid possible. When the Ukrainian Armed Forces liberates or secures an area, they can also secure the circulation of aid to people who need it most. Much of this aid is still distributed through trust-based, civilian networks—such as those networks that were built starting in 2014—but the military plays a necessary role in ensuring the safety of those working to distribute aid, as well as those who receive it.

In other words, the civilian volunteer networks, dominated by women from 2014–2021, have been essential to saving lives since the full-scale invasion in 2022. And they rely on the Ukrainian military, dramatically reformed since 2015, to be most effective. How this will influence women and gender roles in Ukrainian society when the war is over and Ukrainians rebuild their country is an open question. There will be more military veterans trying to return to civilian life than ever before. There will be millions of women and children returning to Ukraine as refugees. We can't yet know what the new post-war Ukraine will look like, but we know that its citizens will take part in rebuilding it together. In the poetic words of Kateryna Iakovlenko, captured in this book, "We are alone in this war. But we are together."

By Oleksandra Matviichuk

Date of birth: October 8, 1983
From: Boyarka, Kyiv region
Profession: Human rights lawyer, director of the Center for Civil Liberties, which was awarded the Nobel Peace Prize 2022
In Kyiv at the start of the invasion

June 15, 2023

I am often asked about the role of women in Russia's large-scale invasion. And I am often at a loss for an answer. I know a lot of fantastic women in a wide variety of fields. Women are making decisions at the state level, women are fighting in the Ukrainian armed forces, women are coordinating volunteer initiatives, and women are documenting war crimes. Women are on the front line in our fight for freedom. Because courage has no gender.

It is difficult for me to answer this question for one simple reason: because a woman can play any role she wants. Every conceivable role belongs to her. And that's precisely what should be the norm. After February 24, many people went to the military police station and joined the territorial defense. Not surprisingly, these people included men. So why should we be surprised that almost sixty thousand women in the Ukrainian armed forces are defending the country with weapons in hand against Russian aggression?

The war against Russia is not simply a war between two states. It is a war between two systems—authoritarianism and democracy. Both have their own values and attitudes.

In the "Russian world," women play only the roles assigned to them in family and society, with men by definition expected to dominate. Authoritarian regimes are based on these cultural principles. The relationships established between men reflect this society's conception of political power. The question is whether there is room for dignity and freedom of choice in relation to state bodies. And what methods of government are acceptable. This is how the personal becomes political. This is why women have the same rights as men in Norway, why women are forbidden to study in Afghanistan, and why domestic violence is decriminalized in Russia—these are always projections of how the government itself treats people in the country concerned.

In this war against Russia, we are also fighting to ensure that our daughters never again have to prove to anyone that they are human beings too.

It is important to hear and understand women's voices in this war. Women have something to say.

[Author's note: For now, Oleksandra Matviychuk and her team will continue to document war crimes so that sooner or later all those who have committed these crimes with their own hands, as well as Putin and his top political leadership and military command, will be held accountable. Together with partners, they have documented more than 81,000 incidents of war crimes. It is important to remember that there is no statute of limitations for international crimes.]

About the Author:

A geopolitician who wrote her doctoral thesis on Gazprom's export strategy to Europe via Ukraine. She has taught at several universities, including Harvard University, where she led a research program on the impact of the global energy transition on traditional oil and gas producers, such as Russia and Iran. She has given numerous conferences, including at MIT and the Université du Québec. In March 2022, she took the decisive step of coordinating an aid project launched by Handelsblatt (Germany's largest financial newspaper) to support Ukrainian journalists, thereby making a definitive departure from research and teaching. Since 2023 she has been writing books and screenplays.

The photographers:

Daria Biliak was born in 1991 in Kyiv. Daria is a Ukrainian photographer and filmmaker living in Berlin since March 2022. From an early age, she loved taking pictures with a small film camera. After graduating as a film and television director from the Kiev National University of Culture and Arts, she moved to Berlin to study at the New School of Photography. Since then she has participated in a number of prestigious national and international projects. She had her first solo exhibition in 2022.

Kristina Parioti was born on September 11, 2002 in Mariupol, Ukraine. A Ukrainian of Greek-Italian origin, she graduated in 2019 and began studying philology at the Mariupol State University, specializing in English and German. During the siege of Mariupol, she and her family went into hiding before fleeing to Germany. She now lives in Ingolstadt, where she is continuing her online studies and starting her career as a photographer. This book is her first international project.

Anastasiia Potapova was born in 1997 in Odesa, where she studied photography. She has been living in Germany since March 2022, where she works as a photographer for various magazines.

Acknowledgements

This book would not have been possible without the support of two exceptional men: My partner, Fabian Gasmia, and Sebastian Matthes, the editor-in-chief at Handelsblatt. Fabian's unconditional love gave me the strength to pull out all the stops. Sebastian gave his confidence und support, allowing me to keep moving forward and hold my course.

My deepest gratitude goes to the three photographers I worked with, Daria Biliak, Kristina Parioti, and Anastasiia Potapova, all the brave participants in this book, who poured their hearts and souls into sharing their stories with passion and dedication, and to the many women who made the publication possible and ensured the book's success: Elisabeth Sandmann, Anne Stukenborg, Katharina Raabe, Silvie Horch, Franziska Günther, Andrea Wasmuth, Deborah Druba, Lily Brett, Mari Kinovych, Alessandra Anzani, Kira Nemirovsky and my dear friends Mariia Shuvalova, Emily Channell-Justice and Mala Emde. Special thanks to Rawi Abdelal and Alexander Abdelal, who moved heaven and earth every time I needed help, and to Christhard Läpple, the Goethe-Institut Ukraine, the Heinrich-Böll-Stiftung, the Friends of the Heinrich-Böll-Stiftung, Handelsblatt's team, Jonathan Landgrebe and Suhrkamp's team especially Ines Lenkersdorf and Demian Sant'Unione, Lana Wachowski, Mstyslav Chernov and Stephen Fry for supporting this project no matter what.

I would like to say a big, heartfelt thank you to Marisa, Toni, Noa, Eden, Ingeborg, Maria, Mandy, Sandhya, Sonia, Olga, Maria, Marie-Dominique, Simon, Paul, and Pierre-Allan, for being there for me through thick and thin.

Finally, I would like to thank everyone who has shown such incredible support for the Ukrainian people. Whether it was through donations, welcoming refugees into their homes, or simply refusing to forget these people in their darkest hour. These small acts of humanity make the world a better place to be.

Photographers:

Cover—Anastasia Potapova
Letter 1:   Olga Stefanyshyna—Kristina Parioti
Letter 2:   Sofia O—Anastasia Potapova
Letter 3:   Olena—Bilozerska Selfie
Letter 4:   Marianna Motrunych—Anastasia Potapova
Letter 5:   Iryna Novokreshchenova—Daria Biliak
Letter 6:   Mariia Lepokhina—Daria Biliak
Letter 7:   Olha Boravlova—Anastasia Potapova
Letter 8:   Jerry Heil—Daria Biliak
Letter 9:   Ira Solomatina—Daria Biliak
Letter 10: Mariia Cherpak—Daria Biliak
Letter 11: Sofiia Kropyvnytska—Anastasia Potapova
Letter 12: Yana Nakonechna—No picture
Letter 13: Adelina Mokliak—Anastasia Potapova
Letter 14: Olga Afanasyeva—Kristina Parioti
Letter 15: Anastasiya Gruba—Anastasia Potapova
Letter 16: Iryna Chernychenko—Kristina Parioti
Letter 17: Kristina Parioti—Daria Biliak
Letter 18: Anastasia Selevanova
Letter 19: Oksana L.—Anastasia Potapova
Letter 20: Olha Olshanska—Kristina Parioti
Letter 21: Maryna Kamenskaya—Kristina Parioti
Letter 22: Kateryna Vozianova—Anastasia Potapova
Letter 23: Taïsia Klochko—Kristina Parioti
Letter 24: Oksana Korchynska—Kristina Parioti
Letter 25: Yuliia Paievska—Kristina Parioti
Letter 26: Sophia Podkolsina—Anastasia Potapova
Letter 27: Meriam Yol—Kristina Parioti
Letter 28: Dina Yong—Anastasia Potapova
Letter 29: Hannah Marholina—No picture
Letter 30: Kateryna Iakovlenko—Kristina Parioti
Analysis 1: Emily Channell Justice—Daria Biliak
Analysis 2: Oleksandra Matviichuk—Kristina Parioti

www.ingramcontent.com/pod-product-compliance
Lightning Source LLC
Chambersburg PA
CBHW061250230426
43663CB00022B/2965